Entrepreneurs Succeed with Us

Creating high performance business

Entrepreneurs Succeed with Us

Creating high performance business

Alan Charlesworth

Matador
9 Priory Business Park
Kibworth Beauchamp
Leicestershire LE8 0RX, UK
Tel: (+44) 116 279 2299
Fax: (+44) 116 279 2277
Email: books@troubador.co.uk
Web: www.troubador.co.uk/matador

ISBN 978 1780885 704

British Library Cataloguing in Publication Data.
A catalogue record for this book is available from the British Library.

Typeset in Helvetica by Troubador Publishing Ltd
Printed and bound in the UK by TJ International, Padstow, Cornwall

Matador is an imprint of Troubador Publishing Ltd

To my dear wife Karen
who makes it all worthwhile

CONTENTS

PREFACE

I was challenged recently to describe what I do.

My first reaction was to discuss the results I get for my clients. The immediate reaction was, 'Yes of course, but I know that. But what do you actually do to achieve these remarkable results?'

This prompted me to think about writing this book.

I have been a CEO of several companies and worked in many others helping entrepreneurs of all sorts, even those hidden away in large corporates, including those in the public sector. None of these roles would have been as successful as they were, without the involvement, motivation, support and capabilities of the people I worked with.

It was inevitable therefore that I would consult with friends, colleagues, associates and clients to agree the key issues facing entrepreneurs and how to provide support for them. The outcome was a commitment to write a book written by a team of practical, experienced business people to provide genuine value to entrepreneurs (especially those already established) who want to improve the performance of their business and achieve their long term goals of expansion or exit.

This book is the result, which we hope very much you will find to be a highly readable set of principles and actions that will convert readily into increased performance and profits in your business.

Each chapter addresses a specific issue such as Marketing, Exit Strategies or Sources of Finance and provides stand-alone advice which can be acted upon immediately within your business.

Other chapters such as 7 Vital Signs or People Development will improve your fundamental knowledge of your business and form the basis for further work and development activity.

Chapters on ICT and the Law are designed to help you avoid unnecessary risks running your business and the chapter on Mindset enables you to improve your own attitude of mind to overcoming problems and grow your business successfully.

My fellow authors (all respected colleagues and good friends) have been the primary inspiration in completing this book and I should like to thank each and every one for their total commitment to the project.

Alan Charlesworth
June 2013

7 VITAL SIGNS

Creating a high performance business

Alan Charlesworth

> There are not enough hours in the day.
> You are dealing with symptoms rather
> than causes and have high levels of
> stress and persistent sleepless nights.

7Vital Signs

Starting your own business is a challenging and rewarding adventure, but it's not long before you realise that it takes on a life of its own. Calling it a living and breathing entity may be going too far, but there is no doubt that it can develop painful and problematic symptoms that need to be understood before you can move forward and fix them.

As an experienced entrepreneur you have steadily expanded your comfort zone and readily identify the issues that concern you and know the buttons to press to counter any negative tendencies in the business.

You might, however, find yourself and your business in one or more of these situations:

- The more successful you have become the more voracious the appetite of your business for more resources, people, overheads, marketing, cash, thinking time, meetings etc.

- You may well be reaching a point where there is discontinuity between where you are today in terms of control of your business and where you would like to be.

The levers you feel you need to pull are bigger, the consequences of the wrong combination of inputs become more serious and the precise decisions you feel obliged to take become less clear.

- The business may have expanded well and has been good to you in terms of profitability and personal reward and wellbeing. Nonetheless there are daily concerns and frustration that are causing you a level of uncertainty, which give you cause for concern because the usual solutions do not seem to work quite as well as they used to.

- After a number of years' success the business has slowly begun to plateau, with sales levelling off and profits in decline as overheads move inexorably upwards. This can be caused by a range of factors, often intermixed, such as new competition, new technology, recession or even a collapse in your market for unexpected reasons. The net effect is that the business has suffered serious setbacks and you may even feel your survival is under threat.

- The resultant effect is a degree of uncertainty about the future and a growing feeling that there are not enough hours in the day. You are constantly dealing with symptoms rather than root causes and experiencing higher levels of stress resulting in persistent sleepless nights.

As a successful entrepreneur you are constantly looking for more time to think about your business and spend time with your family or on leisure pursuits and to avoid the excessive stress which inevitably arises from the day to day pressures in any business. Unfortunately, when you are facing any of the situations described above, or similar ones, this prospect tends to recede ever further into the future.

Achieving these goals requires you to address some of the key fundamentals of your business. You will find though that the need to continue fighting fires and responding to crises does not go away overnight. This chapter is designed to help you narrow down your understanding of the difficulties that afflict your business and begin to focus on relevant solutions. Other chapters provide detailed solutions resulting in the ability to lay the foundations for creating the high performance business you seek.

I have been lucky enough to gain extensive experience at a wide variety of companies, where I have both proposed solutions to difficult situations and acted on them to achieve the desired results.

This process, which has lasted over 20 years, has helped me understand the key underlying and longer-term issues that need to be addressed by any entrepreneur-led company if it is to become a growing and sustainable business.

Addressing the fundamentals of your business is what this book is about. I hope you will find that after you read it you discover a strengthened belief in your ability to create the business of your dreams, which will provide you with the wealth, time and stress-free life to enjoy those rewards.

Summary
My overall conclusions suggest that entrepreneurs can avoid

many of the problems they might encounter if they are more aware of the **7VITALSIGNS** that determine their company's future health, well-being and prosperity. Even if they are unable to avoid all the problems, however, they will have a better idea of how to identify and correct them for the future.

This book is not intended to provide you with a quick fix for your everyday issues. Nevertheless, proper attention to the diagnostic processes and proposed solutions set out in the following chapters, many of which you will be able to implement yourself in conjunction with your management team, should help you to avoid many of the everyday obstacles you face in the future.

Our approach is designed to help you understand the key issues (the **7VITALSIGNS**, as I have christened them), why they are so important, how you can diagnose points at which they might not be functioning correctly and how they can forever be changed for the better by starting an action plan right now.

To enable you to construct this process for yourself I have developed **7VITALSIGNS** which will provide you with reference points and analytical tools to decide where the key issues you face are in the business and to identify solutions and prioritise a plan of action to address them.

Helping you develop a plan

The **7VITALSIGNS** are drawn from my experience of dealing with the problems faced by numerous entrepreneur-led businesses in a variety of industries, all of which have faced problems of market reversal, plateauing growth, profits reversal and competitive pressure, or some combination of these.

The advantage of applying the signs in your business is that you can identify relevant symptoms of decline, convert them to an understanding of the issues concerned and begin to apply solutions in conjunction with your own management team.

They can be summarised as follows:

THE 7VITALSIGNS OF COMPANY PERFORMANCE

1. **Company Vision and Personal Vision**
   Where are you and your company headed?

2. **Managing the Future**
   How should your company be led, managed and developed?

3. **Markets and Customers**
   Have you chosen your markets wisely?

4. **Products and Services**
    Do you have a reputation for quality and innovation?

5. **Strategic Partners**
    Leveraging your company's strengths by forging alliances

6. **Operational and Commercial Risk**
    Anticipate key risk areas in advance

7. **Sources of Finance**
    Financing your business when you need to

The **7VITALSIGNS** are described in more detail in the following pages and their value in understanding the key issues facing your company is explained.

7VITALSIGNS
1. **Company Vision and Personal Vision**

Where are you and your company headed?
Your Vision sets out what you want the business to achieve, be respected and known for and what makes you stand out in your industry. It also defines its values, philosophies, objectives and character. It is different from your own personal vision, why you are an entrepreneur and what exactly you want to achieve for yourself. This has a habit of changing during the life of your business and should be recorded and reviewed as appropriate.

This chapter addresses both these issues in terms of

understanding your business and involving your management team in the process.

Many entrepreneurs founder because they forget that although their success is tied to their business, their preferred outcomes for each might not be the same. You need to prioritise the personal issues you face in determining your future and what you expect from it.

You might eventually sell your business and it could go on to be a global operation, but your personal gain will be your capital exit. You need to decide well in advance.

Let me give you an example of a client I was working with, where the company had plateaued in sales and profits had fallen to a level which threatened its future.

I concentrated on the likely solutions and throughout this process my client did his best, unsuccessfully, to dispose of the company to a trade buyer, both in the UK and overseas. Towards the end of the process, however, which involved considerable consolidation of the company, realignment of management team responsibilities and more focused marketing and sales, the most satisfactory outcome for the client became clear.

One division of the business which turned over about £15 million was making steady profits with hardly any effort at all. It did not, however, interest the owner and I recommended he dispose of it. Its sale would secure the entrepreneur's pension for life, enabling him to retain the rest of the business which he loved as a lifestyle operation. Two years after my assignment, he did just that and re-focused his energy on the rest of the business, which of course became just as dynamic as it had prior to the troublesome period from which I had rescued him.

The thought that he could secure his retirement and retain the business he loved had never occurred to him. If you have seriously thought about your relationship with your business you will have a better idea of what you want from it and when.

7VITALSIGNS
2.   Managing the Future

How should it be led, managed and developed?
As an entrepreneur you set up a business probably because you had a good idea or spotted an opportunity perhaps in a business you are familiar with. The job of course requires you to be an expert in your field, a leader of people, a manager of people and projects, a salesperson and an administrator. How well do you know yourself and how adept have you been at recognising your strengths and weaknesses in recruiting and developing your business?

Have you put in place the skills to develop your long term aspirations for the business?

Recently a seasoned entrepreneur shared with me the lessons learned in his journey from start up to retirement, when he clearly argued that there was no difference between his personal outlook on life and his company Vision.

The entrepreneur in question patented several creative inventions, none of which was commercially successful, so he explored a passion he shared with his father, namely fishing. He designed a range of fly fishing lures, made the moulds and jigs himself and started selling them to some business colleagues. The business developed and in the early 1970s he was awarded a CBI Queen's Award for Export. The inevitable happened of course and overseas competitors (Japanese) entered the market and priced his business out of his worldwide sales. He survived this threat because of his clear philosophy of business.

One of his declared intentions was to provide for his family. Another was that he wanted time both to explore his inventive talents and enjoy some leisure activity. The first restricted his risk taking profile somewhat and probably saved him from bankruptcy more than once during a business life that eventually lasted more than 60 years.

The second had more subtle effects in that he decided to recruit, in the relatively early days of his business, some good managers to undertake the responsibilities that were not his main strengths. This enabled him to focus on developing new products and achieving a work-life balance, while his key team members managed the commercial and operational issues.

Perhaps he missed an opportunity for a significant capital exit. However he successfully cared for his family and maintained a job for life.

7VITALSIGNS

3. Markets & Customers

Have you chosen your markets wisely?
Customers are the lifeblood of any business and a steady supply of high quality customers is essential for future health. How's that for an obvious statement! The issue here is that customers change, competition adapts, channels to market develop, and marketing techniques change in fashion and effectiveness and the basic metrics of sales success are sometime overlooked.

Remember, successful companies turn business away if it doesn't fit their requirements.

There is, however, a simple set of formulae to use to decide whether your marketing and sales effort is adequate.

Number of Leads x Conversion Rate = CUSTOMERS
Customers x Average Value of Sale x Number of Transactions = REVENUE
Revenue x Profit Margin = PROFIT

To determine how you can be more successful with your marketing activities go to Chapter 6 about 'Marketing your business to the next level' and study the 'NINE BOX MATRIX'.

Let me share with you the methods I used at a former employer, in conjunction with an excellent management team. The business enjoyed remarkable growth and a strong reputation in the consumer goods industry for high quality, detailed, regular and comparable reports on most aspects of consumer expenditure.

The reports were very popular with media and services companies and were used for pitch presentations and to help companies looking to enter new markets, as well as larger companies tracking market developments.

New reports were targeted at existing clients and new clients using direct marketing techniques. The extra impact the company generated was through its press and PR coverage which featured in both the national and trade press across all industries. Clients were then interviewed for feedback on reports and the information was directed towards the next report on the same or similar subjects and the improved content featured in future marketing campaigns.

One further boost was to introduce conferences on related subjects, e.g. Grocery Retailing or Consumer Lifestyles, which attracted high calibre delegates from key target customers. This enhanced the company's reputation and its products became 'must haves' for most clients.

With multiple digital channels available now there is no excuse for missing any opportunity to promote both the value of your products and services and their reputation by third party endorsement of all types.

7VITALSIGNS

4.   Products & Services

Do you have a reputation for quality and innovation?

What is your reputation and is it clear to your customers? Have you maintained its integrity throughout your existence? Do you monitor client satisfaction and how you are regarded? A strong reputation will enable you to stretch your brand into new products and related markets, enabling you to take on weaker competition and build your strength and value in the market place.

A client of mine faced severe problems as a result of a recession following a minor boom in the economy. It left the business with serious pressure on profits as it was the dominant force in the market and had large clients to service throughout the country. Overheads, however, were fixed and fees depended on the number of individual clients they provided with their service.

Their business was training and it was delivered by the company on its own premises to major corporates for their staff in order to secure certain qualifications. Fees were already under pressure as many clients were seeking to improve the level of service to their own staff to maintain morale and improve examination pass rates.

It was possible to cut costs by consolidating premises, changing course structures, outsourcing certain services supplied internally such as printing and publishing, introducing more flexible working and working very hard to maintain client satisfaction. It became clear that profits would never be returned to their former level and it was decided to invest a proportion of the money saved into a related training market. This market focused on distance learning, requiring few fixed premises for classrooms, relying more on advertising to gain clients directly and providing them with e-based material and limited face to face tuition.

Such was the company's reputation that within a couple of years it had begun to dominate the new market and was able to acquire the key specialist competition and new management, which resulted in a Management Buyout (MBO) from its corporate owner and a successful future, albeit on a different footing.

7VITALSIGNS

5. Strategic Partners

Leveraging your company's strengths by forging alliances

Many advantages can be gained from negotiating a strategic alliance with another company to improve your business. Most entrepreneurs are reluctant to enter such partnerships because of the inherent risk. The result may end up being one-sided; the day to day operations may not fulfil the ambitions of the senior partners; the results are not as expected or one partner discovers that the other is not to be trusted under certain circumstances. However tangible benefits can be gained which are usually dependent on the quality of the thinking that goes into the setting up of the initial partnership agreement. You need to ensure that you have a good grasp of your objectives for such an arrangement, that they are in keeping with the corporate objectives of your business as well as your own personal vision.

Let us assume that we have some specific objectives in relation to where the business is now and have assessed the future value of the potential access to new technology that has become available. In many if not all circumstances, access to new technology can provide a significant customer benefit and competitive advantage. However, in its early stages of adoption this can prove somewhat intangible until proven and a period of beta testing is essential to prove its potential worth.

An interesting case study from a former employer of mine with a strong brand name illustrates the issue well. In the early days of online publishing the *Financial Times* was beginning to provide access to certain published works online. Despite its obvious pedigree, it felt that the brand offered a solid partnership opportunity in a related field with a broader appeal to a different range of potential corporate and information markets.

My company had been investigating a wide range of partnership opportunities with news providers to deliver either as an additional product to its customers (Mintel's own news service was not technology-based at the time) or as providing access to technology which would otherwise be out of reach. The downside at the time was that most clients did not have good access to the technology and although excited by access to online services (such as they were), were unwilling to pay a premium.

The result of a two year trial was that many clients took both hard copy and online reports and the value of the latter appreciated such that charges were eventually levied. The FT benefited from wider distribution of its service and my company maintained its record of market and product innovation.

7VITALSIGNS
6. Operational and Commercial Risk

The concept of risk management covers a wide range of issues, including the assessment of strategic and operational risk, compliance risk, market risk, credit risk and others. Risk assessment is a subject area not covered, but we do wish to draw your attention to risks with legal and ICT issues that can be overlooked until a problem arises, which is often too late.

There are two chapters in the book devoted to this subject: (Chapter 5 How the law helps your business and Chapter 7 Make technology work for you).

The first deals with the dangers associated with the purchase, implementation and operation of ICT systems. Most entrepreneurs are involved with the day to day running and growth of their business and only start to address technology issues when they go wrong. This can expose you to big risks, such as data loss, non-continuity of business and lack of scalability of systems, i.e., their inability to grow with the company. Identifying and avoiding these mistakes and many others are addressed. How to approach the transition issue of acquiring a custom made ICT system is also covered in some detail.

The second focuses on the legal risks associated with the setting up of a business and the operational issues connected with running it.

If there is more than one partner or an external investor in the business, for example, the shareholder agreement is critical. Employment issues are covered as are the protection of intellectual property, e.g., copyright, patents etc., contract risk, as well as many of the key elements to be aware of and ensuring you have access to the best advisers at the appropriate time.

The biggest risk entrepreneurs often take is the failure to seek the right advice for a given situation. They are so used to taking charge themselves that they put themselves and their businesses at risk in this way far too often.

7VITALSIGNS

7.   Sources of Finance

Financing your business when you need to

I recently attended a meeting where a bank manager outlined the criteria his bank use to assess the creditworthiness of a potential company client for a bank loan.

It went by the acronym CAMPARI defined below, and in itself the acronym clearly explains, to me at least, why it is so difficult to get a loan for a new project from a clearing bank.

C haracter and personal statements

A bility and track record

M eans to repay and collateral available

P urpose and legality

A mount. Can it be justified and may need more information

R epayment and profitability of the business

I nsurance. What happens if something goes wrong?

This is why we have tried in this book to introduce you to a wider range of sources of finance for your business depending on your specific requirements.

It does not need me to remind you that with so many assurances required it is almost impossible to get a clean sheet agreement, which emphasises the value of the quality of your relationship with the bank. This is all very well of course but your account manager often changes, the lending criteria change, even for existing overdrafts and the requirements of new liquidity ratios imposed on banks means they are less free now than ever to lend.

See Chapter 4, Sources of finance to grow your business, to help you explore the wide range of alternatives available.

THE VALUE OF SLEEPLESS NIGHTS

Before you are able to draw conclusions about your business it is vital to collect as much information as you can from the perspective which is uniquely your own.

Only you have lived with and created this business to the extent of its current success and you have a personal relationship with it for which there is no substitute.

Below I propose the use of a **7VITALSIGNS DASHBOARD** to collect information about company performance not readily available from the usual channels.

- You will already have in place conventional measures of your company's performance, for example, sales, debtors, creditors, forward orders etc. Your accountant tells you how much profit you are making; you appraise your staff annually. However, the measures which are more difficult to monitor are those that keep you awake at night or trouble you in the shower, or suddenly hit you in the middle of an important meeting.

- These are the sudden insights which may not have an obvious cause, but worry you nonetheless. For example, in a client meeting there is a comment on poor quality or late delivery or perhaps about a competitor's product, which the client claims to have mentioned before with no result.

   The normal and obvious response is to pull a member of staff to one side and grill them on the issue raised. This may well produce a satisfactory answer but do you, as a result, get to the root of the problem? It's easy to move on to the next problem and perhaps overlook the more fundamental significance of the issues raised.

- The second step, now that you have accepted your business as a living organism which needs to be treated as such, is to monitor its progress through your own observation. Become your own company doctor no less. The best place to start is with your own concerns, observations, frustrations and worries.

Instead of simply allowing them to keep you awake at night, see if you can capture them in a **7VITALSIGNS DASHBOARD** so that after a month or so signs of a pattern will emerge. You can then begin to relate symptoms to causes which can be converted into action both for immediate effect and longer term benefit.

As well as completing the **7VITALSIGNS DASHBOARD** daily, it is also a good idea to make more general observations about the company and its performance and some of the longer term or strategic issues that concern you.

Here's an example of a **7VITALSIGNS DASHBOARD** to use for 7 days. Most entrepreneurs never forget their company and ideas and issues may arise at any time, even in the middle of the night.

**The layout makes it easy enough to jot down your thoughts as they come to you.
The only decision to make is to which category each should be assigned.**

This can easily be left until a more appropriate moment when a true perspective can be gained on the cause of your sleeplessness.

Completing the chart each week will help bring out the issues that concern you.

At first you might only have two or three thoughts each day while you get used to the idea.

In my experience a pattern will emerge and you will be able to categorise your thoughts into a table (in soft or hard copy) similar to that opposite in Chart 1, with many more entries.

CHART 1: 7VITALSIGNS DASHBOARD   EXAMPLE

7VITALS IGNS	No 1 Vision	No 2 Manage-ment	No 3 Custom-ers/ Markets	No 4 Products /Services	No 5 Partners	No 6 Opera-tional and Commer-cial Risk	No 7 Finance
Day 1	Where's the sense of achievement gone? It seems to be all problems and stress						
Day 2		People huddled in corners. Do I know what's troubling them?					
Day 3			Sales are complaining of a lack of leads. Are there enough of the right calibre?				
Day 4				When we started customers used to come to us with new ideas; now they tell us about competitive products.			
Day 5					Why is the competition first with this new technology? I thought we were the innovators.		
Day 6						Why is so much time spent on this customer? Does this mean they are unprofitable?	
Day 7							We are still growing but seem to have less cash and make less profit.

The next stage is to assess the information collated over days, weeks or months and introduce some interpretation. This will enable a sense of control over your understanding of the business problems you face and ultimately an ability to move forward towards some solutions.

There is no limit to the amount of data you can analyse, provided the grouping is clear and the implications fully thought through.

CHART2: 7VITALSIGNS DASHBOARD INTERPRETATION

7VITALSIGNS	No 1 Vision	No 2 Management	No 3 Customers/ Markets	No 4 Products/ Services	No 5 Partners	No 6 Operational & Commercial Risk	No 7 Finance
Dashboard Note	Where's the sense of achievement gone? It seems to be all problems and stress	People huddled in corners. Do I know what's troubling them?	Sales are complaining of a lack of leads. Are there enough of the right calibre?	When we started customers used to come to us with new ideas; now they tell us about competitive products.	Why is the competition first with this new technology? I thought we were the innovators.	Why is so much time spent on this customer? Are they becoming less profitable?	We are still growing but seem to have less cash and make less profit.
Interpretation	Are all the problems coming to your door? Are you the key decision maker because your management is not strong enough to deal with as many issues as you'd like.	Perhaps you should talk to people more. Have your managers noticed? What's their view of the causes?	How effective is marketing at generating leads from the right prospects? Are we on top of social media developments and the latest SEO techniques?	Innovation comes in all guises, from clients, overseas, new technology and academia. How well are we keeping up?	Is it our expertise which has lagged behind or our ability to invest? Is there a University which could help us?	Has it become too important to us and are they exploiting our dependence on them?	Many companies measure success by cash flow. You can use it to repay debt, invest in new projects, and acquire other companies, or fund partnerships.

WHAT ACTION DO YOU TAKE?

For certain you will not have the range of issues all neatly collated, but you will have a collection of genuine concerns which have arisen from the things you worry about daily.

Categorise them as best you can as shown above under each of the **7VITALSIGNS** headings and apply some weight to them so that you can prioritise them.

- If you have a concern about your personal vision, why not jot down what you think it should be (use the chapter on Exit Strategies as a guide), discuss it with your partner, your accountant or other trusted advisor/friend and then park it for future reference. Unless of course it has suddenly become imminent, in which case get on with it more rapidly.

- If it's the company vision that worries you then that is probably a top priority as without it, it can be difficult to motivate everyone into the future.

- If you feel strong in your market and your intention is rapid expansion then a strong product portfolio is a priority, together with the finance and potential partners to back it up.

- If the market you have worked so hard to develop is slipping away from you, restorative action is needed to re-establish your position and reputation in this market; otherwise you will not have an adequate foundation on which to build your business for the future.

You need to establish the key issues to address first and you might end up with something like Table 3.

TABLE 3: 7VITALSIGNS DASHBOARD   ACTION PLAN

7VITALSIGNS	Issue	Priority	Timetable
1. VISION	Clarity of Vision	High	Immediate
2. MANAGEMENT	Marketing/Sales Management weak	High	6 months
3. CUSTOMERS	Market/share decline	High	Immediate- 6 months
4. PRODUCTS	No portfolio	Medium	One year
5. PARTNERS	Low innovation	Medium	One year
6. RISK	Overheads too high	Medium	One year
7. FINANCE	Invest in re-launch	Medium	One year

- This demonstrates quite clearly the value of recording and categorising the issues that concern you over a relatively short period of time.

- It enables you to identify the main action points and gives you some very clear projects to work on with your team and enables you to consult with external help on issues already identified.

- You will find it also gives you more confidence in developing your business into the future and a modus operandi to review your business, even before the sleepless nights begin all over again.

Alan says:

Clearly you can discover for yourself the reasons for your company's underperformance. This leads to the next step which is to decide the priorities for action.

Which areas should you address to have the quickest and most profound effect on improving company profits?

Follow this with a plan of action for at least the next 12 months and as before taking on board your management team for total commitment.

My 20 years' experience of helping businesses understand more fully how they can achieve above average growth or resolve seemingly intractable problems suggests that many of the solutions are often internally available.

The 7VITALSIGNS DASHBOARD helps provide an insight into the problems you face and the necessary action to resolve them.

The important issue is to understand the underlying problems through examination of the symptoms and assessing the relevant solutions. It is remarkable how quickly a renewed focus on causes and opportunities can provide a new perspective on the future. The key is to take the time out to look ahead with a more analytical approach.

It's also worth thinking about how often and for how long you have given yourself the opportunity to think clearly about what you want to achieve. What has prevented you in the past from deciding on and taking necessary action?

The authors, as experienced business people themselves, hope that you will find this book useful in prioritising problems and helping you find the solutions you need. We are always on hand for advice on a no commitment basis should you wish to seek clarification of any aspect of this book.

DEVELOP YOUR PEOPLE TO DRIVE YOUR STRATEGY

Maurice Cheng

> You will have an empowered management team, and a well managed, engaged and supportive staff, all working towards a common Vision.

Developing your people to drive your strategy

You've built your own company; it's been growing nicely and doing well. Your vision for the product or service you offer has come right, and you have happy customers and contented staff. You've put in long hours, stayed on top of all key aspects of running and managing your company activities, and have a small number of key loyal staff – managers – who have grown up with you and the company. You deservedly take great pride from what you've achieved and built.

The main frustration is that growth has tailed off over the last few years, and you've tried new products, and hired and fired a few new staff who should have been able to bring new skills and perspective, but growth is inconsistent and slow. The other main frustration is that a lot of the new people you've been bringing on board – and even the people that have been with you for several years – need a lot of personal supervision and management, and you wish you had more time to devote to thinking about how to restart growth, and getting on with these development initiatives.

This chapter is about your people, and some ideas about how to support them to support you. This will not be a comprehensive look at the vast and complex area of Human Resource strategy, but aims to highlight and explain a number of key initiatives which have worked for me and my clients over the years.

The key objective in undertaking these initiatives is aligning your people and their skills with what you and your company need to move forward and grow robustly and sustainably. Your staff are no doubt a wonderful bunch, but they are a collection of individuals with a range of personal ambitions, skills and views of what is happening and what will happen at work. 'Aligning' or 'engaging' with your staff is not about trying to brainwash them into 'living the company', but about maximising your chances to bring about a tight team, giving them the opportunity to bring their best skills into play, and getting their support for building the company by encouraging and listening to their ideas about how the future should happen.

I've set out over the course of this chapter a seven step programme of how you could go about this. You might not need all these steps, and may want to change the order in which you tackle them, so do use these in whatever way fits your specific circumstances – and do talk to your team about this!

I – Build a Vision for the future with your managers

Building a clear, commonly understood vision for where your company is going is the bedrock for the development of the organisation and your people. Where you want to get to is a description of a target state that you and your team feel you can get to, which then gives you clarity about building the plans that will get you there.

Which you've probably been doing anyway with your partners or directors in the business for some time – but this time try it with all the managers, or managers and team leaders, or indeed everyone if your headcount isn't that high. Plan on having workshop sessions – probably two or three – where you can all understand the environment you operate in, the challenges and opportunities you face, and together look at crafting the goal state – the Vision – for your company. I would recommend that however many people you decide to engage in these strategic planning sessions, keep to a maximum of around 10 per group. More than this starts getting unwieldy and risks having people unengaged with the process.

My advice on these strategic planning groups is – share what you already know and what's in your head, but also make sure your base information is comprehensive and based on evidence rather than conjecture. Prepare briefing notes – even better, get your participants to prepare key factsheets – and allow time in the first part of the workshop for all the participants to understand and assimilate the information provided. This process isn't about you sharing what you already know and getting others to agree with it, it's your opportunity to let others get involved in your company's future, and give you their thoughts as well as understand yours.

So prepare solid background information on customer needs; competitive activity; economic and political environment; distribution channels, customer satisfaction reports and so on. If you've already done an analysis of your company's Strengths, Weaknesses, Opportunities and Threats put that in the mix too; also anything you may have done by way of a Risk Register, historical P&L information, latest management accounts. This looks a lot but you should have most or all of this information anyway, and bringing it all together for the purposes of strategic planning will be time very well spent.

In your strategy workshop sessions, start by emphasising that this is a 'safe' environment to think and plan in: there are no stupid questions, no stupid ideas, all points of view will be looked at and assessed on their merits. Also emphasise that all discussions within the workshop are confidential, as a corollary to that freedom of thought and expression. Spend as much time as you need with your participants developing an understanding of the background information and evidence you have, and only then start on the next phase, defining where you could take the company next, and by when.

Share your ideas with your team, but also give them the space and time to come up with their ideas, their interpretations. Ultimately the Vision of the company is your call, and there's nothing wrong in gently steering the conclusions towards your own strongly held views, but this process of opening up to informed idea generation about what the company's goals and timescales could be from all your managers and workshop participants, and encouraging them to challenge and understand each other's views, will give you much deeper buy-in and real understanding of the way forward. By all means use breakout group techniques in your workshops – splitting up into smaller discussion units to focus on different or identical issues, then coming back together to present the results of these in plenary – to encourage even better participation by all team members. It's the investment in shared thinking time that brings dividends – even if you do end up with a Vision that you personally started with! And if, as often happens, you end up somewhere different, that makes better sense, then that's a huge win too.

What you should be working towards is a clear description of target goal or target state for your company within a defined timescale – the classic example of such is NASA's 'We will put a man on the moon in 10 years'. If you are able to derive a commonly agreed practical Vision by the end of your two or three sessions, tremendous. If you don't – and quite often there are lots of possible scenarios that look attractive, or information that is needed to reach a decision – use the workshops to inform your next steps to reach that needed conclusion. The important thing is to have a clear process and deadline by which this new corporate Vision should be finalised, so that all the participants and all the other members of staff appreciate that such 'engagement' processes have a real purpose and real deliverables.

This approach of getting your corporate vision clear – and using a collaborative approach so that your people contribute and buy into it – really does pay dividends, and often quite quickly. One of my clients, who owned and ran a publishing and events company, was finding it very difficult to get consistent growth, despite a barrage of new ideas and new initiatives which were introduced constantly. We worked with her co-directors and senior managers to build a broader and deeper analysis of the market and the trading environment than she had previously undertaken, and from this built a framework of new perspectives and understanding about customer need and motivation – resulting in a clear, time mapped definition of vision. Two years on, annual growth is over twenty percent and rising.

If you're in the not for profit or charity field, the creation of a strong and evidence based vision can bring immediate dividends. Any professional fundraiser will tell you how critical the formulation of an inspirational case for support is to a fundraising campaign, and this works on an organisational level too. A few years ago, as the interim CEO of a professional association in the health sector, I guided the trustee Board to build a clear Vision for the organization, which I then used to gain policy and funding support from the NHS and commercial partners – about £500,000 was raised in six months on this basis.

II – From Vision to Action

Now that you – and your senior managers – have worked out a clear Vision for the future, the real strategic planning starts. Work out the key strategies that will get you from where you are now – also referred to as the 'As Is' position – to the end state described as the 'To Be' position. Your Vision timeline probably works over three to five years, so work out your strategies over that period – don't (as is very tempting) try to plan for everything to be done in the first year. Make sure the strategies actually do add up to the work programme you need to deliver your Vision, and that the strategies work in synergy with each other in terms of dependencies (some projects will have to deliver before others), resources (people and finance) and timing.

I recommend you rough out the core strategies with a small core team of managers – ideally the same group that participated in the Vision workshops – and then delegate the detailed working of each strategic work-stream down to individual project leads, with the intention of engaging with their teams or peers in the specific design of the strategy. This way, you start to spread out the involvement in the strategic planning process early, with more people, and you will end up with much better understanding of where and how the organisation is developing.

What I often do with clients is use a mindmap approach to sketch out the strategies, starting with the Vision in the centre of its surrounding strategies and plans. If your Vision was to, say, become the most profitable company in your sector over the next five years, what would the three to five core strategies be? They could be, for example, improving productivity; innovating high margin products; improving brand presence and image; become a fun supportive place to work, and so on. Each of these would then become the centre of its own mindmap, with three to five contributory sub-strategies that go up to deliver the key objectives. And each of these third tier strategies could have its own sub-strategies, and so on.

If you lay these out so that you start with the Vision on the left hand side of a large sheet of paper, and set out the first 'tier' of strategies just to the right of that Vision, and the second tier of sub-strategies to the right of these, and so on, you will end up with a classic strategic tree diagram (although I always think it looks more like a root system, whatever works for you!). You now have an interlinked set of strategies and plans, probably four or five layers deep, all devoted towards delivering the company Vision. You will find a number of the actions link to or coincide with each other, and will need to acknowledge these links and overlaps in your detailed planning.

With this mindmap as the visual blueprint, your next step is to break it down into annual chunks – which actions take place when? – which should basically give you the core of your business plans for the next three to five years. No longer will business plans just be 'last year but a bit better' – they become part of an integrated plan to deliver your strategic Vision.

One common outcome of this focussed approach to building your corporate strategy – focussed, that is, on delivering your agreed Vision – is that there are often activities that don't fit. These activities could be anything from an internal process, to a whole range of products and services – the opportunity however is that you should ask yourselves, if this doesn't fit the Vision, is it worth doing? Could the resources expended on this activity be better expended on delivering the Vision better, or faster? These decisions could be quite tough, particularly if they could involve stopping something which has been done for some time, but even if you decide to continue with the activity, you now have the additional perspective that it might need to be changed to fit in with your strategy, or it may point to your strategy needing to be tweaked in some way.

One public sector organisation I work with had this dilemma, in that its secondary but significant activity area – offering family oriented health and fitness programmes – wasn't an immediately obvious fit with its newly defined Vision of building truly integrated support programmes for homeless young people. At the end of the day they decided not to stop providing these health and fitness programmes, but actually to work towards integrating these into the rehabilitation programmes for disadvantaged young people – by training them in how to be gym instructors, for example – which actually strengthened the delivery of the corporate Vision.

III – Right people, right skills, right places

You've now got your corporate Vision in place, and the strategies for getting there have been drawn up. While the strategic plans were being discussed, you've also been working out the budget and costs for the plans and workstreams. It would be appropriate at this stage to also do a review of the skills in the organisation, and identify where you may need to develop or bring in specific skills and experience to ensure that the strategies are delivered.

It's a good approach to start with a clean sheet and set out what company structure would best support the delivery of your Vision – and if this turns out to be very similar to your current structure, all well and good. In this 'blank sheet' structure, set out the key roles – directors, managers, team leaders, the number of people in their teams – and take care to define in detail what key skills each role should have.

And remember, management is also a key skill set – and not one which is automatically gifted to high performance specialists in specific fields. Your best salesman may not necessarily make your best sales manager – so do think about where you may need management skills improved also.

This may be relatively simple to spot – are there any particular departments or teams where you have to step in more often than others? Are there any managers who seldom, if ever, come to you with ideas or suggestions for improvements? Which managers promise a lot and tend not to deliver on time or to expectation? You might reflect on whether the need for management skill may even start with you yourself: one partnership I worked closely with realised when they got to this stage of considering key skills that actually it was the partners' lack of strong management that was a key block to progress, and they specifically recruited strong and experienced managers as part of the new people mix.

When you do this draft restructure, do start with key structures and key roles – not people's names. Once you have the right roles in the right places (and do be realistic about the level of skills each role will need to have), then start to populate the structure with names – and again, do be realistic about whether an individual (favourite or not) has a particular skill and level of expertise. If specific individuals don't fit, think whether they can and should be developed into specific roles through training or coaching, or placed in roles different from their current one, or whether – rather harshly perhaps – they might need to be managed out.

Once you've reviewed and decided on your ideal corporate structure, identified your skills and people gaps, and have a plan for what to do about filling these, you may be heading into the realm of a formal restructure. Restructuring an organisation is not something that should be undertaken lightly, but despite the employment law minefield that is involved, if the process is justifiable (i.e., the restructure serves a genuine business need) and managed by the book (so do make sure you have the right HR and employment law specialists on board to help), you can actually achieve what you need – at some cost – which is putting the right people in the right places to drive your company.

IV – Communications strategy – the glue between people

One of the key workstreams in any strategy is internal communications, and one which is often ignored or downplayed in smaller companies. When there were only a few of you in the company, communications seemed easy – everyone 'just knew' everything. When there were only one or two dozen in the whole organization, it's still pretty easy to have everyone in a meeting room at the same time. When staff numbers grew beyond that, communicating information from the boss down to all staff tends to evolve into some form of information cascade through the managers – although I have also seen some rather appalling examples where internal communications came via email 'from the desk of the Chief Executive'. Inspiring it wasn't!

It's at the stage where you can't easily get all your staff into the same room that a formal internal communications strategy is critical. Particularly if you're trying to implement a new Vision and growth strategy, and bring all the staff along with you.

The reason why I'm not recommending email based communications alone is that it's very impersonal, it's one directional, and unless you have the writing style of Stephen Fry, email newsletters are unlikely to have the inspirational impact you're looking for. Electronic communications can be very useful in this context as support channels, and intranets, online forums, Instant Messenger protocols, even Twitter can help to improve communications, but I would strongly advocate good old fashioned face to face meetings as the core mechanism, to show your leadership and that of your managers, and allow the building of a responsive and interactive relationship between you and your staff.

What has worked well for me and my clients over the years is to set up formal one to one meetings with your top tier managers, with a formal regular agenda of items which you can share information about, on a weekly or fortnightly basis – this is on top of whatever casual or 'walkabout' chats you may have on a daily basis. Your managers should be encouraged to have the same with their top team, and so on down the line. On a monthly basis, bring your top team together for a formal monthly meeting – again, with a formal agenda, and action minutes from the session. This need not take very long (although the first few may take half a day as your managers settle down to understanding what each other does), but is an invaluable touchpoint to share information, progress and challenges, and very importantly, celebrate success. Again, your managers should be encouraged to have regular team sessions with their groups. I always recommend that one of the standing agenda points of the various team meetings is about what information should be transmitted either up or down the line – and if you can get this working properly, you get a fantastic two way information cascade.

Cap this series of team based meetings with a full company meeting – every one to three months, depending on practicality and need – and you will have a pretty effective internal communications engine running. Then you can add in email, intranets, online groups etc. to complement this, to focus attention on specific issues.

I know this must seem a lot of effort and time expenditure – and you will get a lot of comments about 'yet another meeting' – but investment in communication time with and between your staff will help to build stronger working relationships, increased respect for other people's roles and challenges, and a stronger sense of understanding of what is going on, and where you all are along the road to delivering that target Vision. The time investment is critical as a key part of ongoing performance management, of which more later.

I've been using this people communications approach for nearly twenty years, and the outcomes are really quite impressive. At one of my latest companies, which started with deep divisions between departments, high levels of absence and sickness, and a long seated general mood of 'directors vs the staff', this use of constant and consistent two way communication – as was evidenced by an annual staff survey that I implemented – showed a rising understanding of where the company was going, greater confidence in management and in each other, increasing willingness to share information and ideas with each other, and lower levels of sickness and absence.

On the other hand, I have observed a recently appointed chief executive who shied away from promoting and leading the internal communications process, experience a rash of senior management resignations within a space of eighteen months of joining, as staff became less and less engaged with what was going on, and the good ones found it preferable to jump ship, even in the middle of an economic downturn.

V – Getting the people basics right

So, you involved lots of staff in building your Vision, you have a strategic plan which will deliver, you are clear about what people and skills you need to get you there (and a roadmap of how), and you and your managers are now communicating better with each other and all down to the most junior member of staff. A quick check-up on your HR basics would be really useful at this point; you're embarking on an extended period of significant change (particularly if you are considering a restructure as part of the mix), and need to make sure your staff are with you. The HR basics are regarded as a hygiene factor by many smaller business owners, but are critically important in terms of staff morale and the relationship the staff have with the company. Think about what your staff would think about you and your company if they were paid one day late. Think how terrible it would be if it happened more than once.

The sort of 'HR Basics' checklist I recommend you look at include:

1. Is the Staff Handbook up to date with current legislation and current practices inside the company?

2. Are your HR policies – including remuneration – clear, up to date, and consistently applied?

3. Are your employee records (including sickness and holidays) accurate?

4. What is your payroll error rate? There will be errors, but is it enough to cause concern (to employees, not you!)? Late pay days by the way is the WMD of payroll errors.

5. Do you have effective staff complaints handling? This is also important if anything goes wrong in the relationship with an individual and employment law is triggered in some form.

You might also need to re-evaluate the level of HR expertise you have in the company – if your concerns are about taking your company into the next phase of growth with more than 20 people you probably need to get an experienced HR consultant in to support the more junior HR officer resource that you've probably been using – certainly to look at and update the five process issues I've outlined above, and to help you deliver the higher level challenges such as restructuring.

The costs of getting your people basics right may cause a little intake of breath – two companies I have experience of which had outdated policies and HR support structures had to spend over £60,000 over a couple of years to address this properly – but this should be compared with the potential costs of getting it wrong. One of these two – in which I stepped in as CEO – had laid out over £150,000 in the previous two years as a result of not having up to date and watertight HR policies and processes. A lot of this was wasted in settling spurious employment tribunal cases. I know that the current government is trying to address and simplify some of these employer liability issues, but whatever changes may happen will take time to work through the system – so don't leave yourself exposed if you are already.

VI – Managing performance

I find pretty often that clients assess the performance of their staff either through achievement of short-term goals – the monthly sales target, for example – or specific objectives and tasks, and management is almost entirely 'by walkabout' – along the lines of 'hello, how's this going, great, carry on'. There's nothing wrong with going walkabout and finding out what's going on, but effective management of performance, and getting the best out of your people, is creating a formal understanding about what is required from them, and from you to them in terms of support in their role. Then to build on this understanding through regular – and formal – reviews of how both sides are doing in this arrangement.

Performance management is an approach used to define and control this type of arrangement, and in the context where you and your managers (with the assistance of the rest of the staff) have clearly defined the company's Vision, then set out the strategies, broken down by period (e.g., each financial year's milestones), it is a relatively straightforward task then breaking these project and activity outcomes down to team and individual responsibilities. And if you have already built your clear vision, strategy and plan, then these individual and team objectives that arise from them will almost certainly be more than sales targets and a string of specific tasks.

Once you and your managers have this level of detail embedded in your strategic and annual business plans, you can then use these target outcomes in team and individual targets and plans for the year – the managers get the team targets, and the team members get defined subsets as theirs.

Where these team and personal objectives get used is at the annual appraisal meetings – an important part of the performance management process. My experience is that many owner managers let such formal reviews of performance slip in time and importance, working on the assumption that day to day contact with managers is enough of a control mechanism.

The benefits of moving to a more formal process of regular review is that you can make a more objective evaluation of how well an individual member of staff is performing against set (and agreed) criteria – and can then do something about it. This replaces the more typical slightly fuzzy view of how an employee is doing based on the most recent good or bad thing that they did.

My recommendation is that you institute formal appraisals for all your staff at a period in the year (financial year) where you have a good idea of how well the company and they have performed over the last year, and after you and your top team have agreed the business plan for the following year, so that the objectives for departments, teams and individuals are already clear.

All staff should get an appraisal, however senior or junior, each person with his or her line manager. Both appraisee and appraiser should spend some time preparing for the appraisal meeting, to make the session as objective and useful as possible. The discussion should go through a standard appraisal form that both have contributed to, and the appraiser's comments and conclusions about the appraisee's performance should be given at the meeting, reflected in an annual written record as part of the appraisal form, and the whole document signed by both appraiser and appraisee. This way you have a solid record of a fair and objective performance review meeting, and over time, a series of such documents which accurately reflect how well an individual has been performing. Do make sure that all appraisals are not only undertaken, but the written and signed appraisal forms sent back into HR within a strictly enforced time period, otherwise both appraisals and the record will slide as other priorities come up through the year.

The appraisal form – the backbone of the appraisal meeting – should have the appraisee's objectives for the prior year (the period being being appraised) set out clearly, and the appraisee should fill out his/her comments about progress against each of these, and send the form to the appraiser so that a response can be prepared.

Another useful section would be to set out the half dozen or so core competences (skills) which the role that the individual holds should perform well at – for example, people management, communications, initiative/creativity would be key for most managers. Again, the appraisee should fill out this section to send to the appraiser in advance of the meeting.

The next and critical section is a discussion around what

objectives should be set for the next period (i.e., new financial year) – the appraisee, who will (of course) have been involved in contributing to the new year's business plan and has a copy of it, should contribute initial ideas again for advance sending to the appraiser.

The last section that I have always found useful in appraisal discussions, should form a part of the appraisal form to be prefilled, is a review of the usefulness of any training that has been undertaken in the previous year, and a proposed training plan (or PDP – Personal Development Plan) for the next year. As the discussion progresses about the performance of the individual, it should become more clear what additional skills development and training may be required to help the individual perform to expectation in the following year, and these actions (sometimes called interventions in the professional training world) should be set out in the PDP.

And that's about it. Appraiser and appraisee ideally should spend an hour or so preparing for their meeting, mainly in filling out the relevant sections of the appraisal form, and the meeting should be objective, focussed and interactive (I always ask my appraisee what they thought of my management at the same time – a good opportunity for feedback!). The standard advice is not to discuss remuneration at all during the appraisal, otherwise the focus on performance could be rapidly derailed once reward comes into the frame. Just remember, the overall objective of performance management appraisals is to get an objective and practical appraisal of how well a member of staff is performing, and what help he or she needs to continue to perform and grow in the role. It is not *per se* about assigning blame for things that have gone wrong over the last year – such feedback should be given, if appropriate and supported by evidence, at the time the poor performance occurred, not months later at an annual review.

I would personally also implement a mid-year appraisal meeting using the agreed appraisal form and objectives for the year, so that any performance issues can be picked up and corrected early, but depending on the load on your managers this may not always be practical.

VII – Building your top team – and letting go the reins

The last key initiative I recommend to owner managers is – plan to let go, and build a strong management team that can help deliver the Vision, and drive growth and continuity in the future. Particularly if one of your key life goals is to find an exit and sell off your company at some point, you will anyway need to sell it as an organisation with strong managers – without you, in time.

We touched on the benefits of evaluating the people, skills and structure you needed to deliver your corporate Vision, and as part of that process you should look at the management expertise you will need – and when you will need it – so that at an appropriate point you are replaceable. You may not need to put in high level management skills today, but whenever that appropriate time is, you should have a clear idea about how you plan to develop that resource – hire in, or develop an existing promising member of staff? If you need a rapid injection of these skills for specific projects now, consider the use of interims to help you kickstart that particular programme.

If you have put in place the structures and programmes outlined above, you should have the basis of good communication and performance management across your and other management tiers, and have already started to move people into the right places where they can develop and be more effective.

One of the last key pieces of this pretty extensive change programme therefore is you, and the way in which you manage your top team. Do you still insist on making every major decision on product, pricing, sales strategy, procurement and so on? If you are still making all the key decisions, is it because your senior team don't have the skills and experience to make the right calls, or because you haven't let them?

Appropriate and managed delegation of authority will probably be an uncomfortable journey if you are an owner manager used to making all the key calls, but one which you will need to embark upon so that your increasingly competent top team (assuming you are putting that in place) is empowered and able to take over the day to day running of the company. I do meet a fair number of owner manager clients who indeed complain that the day to day running of the company is dull, and they wish they could spend more time planning for the future – but at the same time still insisting on controlling every key decision.

Giving new delegated powers to current managers, or ceding such authority to newly recruited senior managers, needs to be done with clarity and precision – what these are, where the boundaries are, what they should do if they want to do something beyond the boundaries. The regular one to one meetings that you will of course have set up become critical to ensuring that delegation goes well, and that any problems are aired and solved quickly and effectively.

You may find it useful to bring a business coach on board for a period – probably three to six months – to help you think through how you start to move decision making from you to your team over time. Someone who has no vested interest, and who can be a neutral sounding board on the issues you face with individual managers or specific issues, can be very helpful indeed.

One other tactic that I have found helpful is the use of teambuild training – whether it involves crossing imaginary chasms on planks, yomping up snowclad hills giving each other feedback in freezing conditions, or doing a Sandhurst assault course, you do find that the mood and relationship shift is significant and very tangible for a while – and if mixed into your battery of change programmes, will very much help to create new working perspectives and create new workstyles. I have actually been on a teambuild programme where, towards the end of a three day programme which involved climbing up and standing on top of freezing Welsh hills, one of my colleagues decided that she really wanted to tell the chief executive exactly what she thought of him, and did so loudly, in front of the rest of us, and standing on a mound of snow. Interestingly the key benefit coming from this outburst was that, with the professional barriers down for the first time between them, there developed a far better understanding of how to deal with each others' strengths and weaknesses.

Most of these programmes I have outlined in this chapter involve activities which many smaller (and indeed quite a few larger) companies do sporadically, or not at all. They all involve time investment, and at the beginning, significant amounts of it. Even after this gets underway, you will probably find you are spending around 15-20% of your and your senior managers' time supporting and maintaining all these people-related programmes.

The payoff however is that you will have an empowered management team, and a well managed, engaged and supportive staff, all working towards a common Vision, with a clear plan and timeline. A lot of the frustration about not being able to achieve a target future will be gone, and you will have a mechanism to monitor and adjust your plans along the way, working in concert with your new best friends – your top team.

Alan says:

It's obvious that your Vision for the company is vital to its future health and the total commitment and motivation of everyone involved with it. It will continue to absorb most of your time and energy for the foreseeable future.

Don't forget, however, that although your company has been your life for some years it is also a healthy option for you to consider your own personal mission, especially the satisfaction you get from the company and the future rewards you expect.

You will see from other chapters in this book that your own personal performance as a leader and Chief Executive can also be enhanced, helping you to be even more successful and happier in your role. Perhaps giving you the chance to gain more time, and suffer less stress from the role.

An exit from the company is an issue to be considered right now if you have not done so already as it takes time to develop the right circumstances, including company valuation, before you can expect this to be successfully negotiated.

DEVELOPING YOUR ENTREPRENEURIAL MINDSET

Suzanne Hazelton

The mindset, attitude and skills that got you to where you are today may not take you to where you want to go.

Developing your entrepreneurial mindset

Introduction

One of the key things that can hold a person back in achieving further business success is their mindset. As Henry Ford said, "*Whether you think you can or think you can't you're right*". Sadly, self-sabotaging thoughts can all too easily get in the way of you achieving your success.

Mindset can become fixed if you think you already have all the answers. However, to advance through the different stages of business leadership, you will have to learn new and different skills at each stage. We shall first explore the stages of leadership then examine the qualities and benefits of an open mindset. If you look for all the ways something won't work, you're sure to find them, but in doing so you will begin to attract them. The antidote is to look for opportunities; not only will you be constantly on the lookout for opportunities, but your mind will be open and **expecting** to see them.

Adopting a 'growth mindset', the opposite of a fixed mindset, often means learning and changing. Many people assume that learning is a switch – you either know something or you don't. However, there is a process of learning which when you're learning can be frustrating. Since many people quit at the first hurdle, if you persevere through the tough bits it will begin to set you apart and help you advance further and faster.

We also examine the importance of having a long term vision and the setting and achieving of goals in order to achieve both personal and business results. Finally, the chapter will close by exploring why you should invest in positive emotions – and the personal and business benefits of ensuring you have a smile on your face.

What type of business leader are you currently?

There are stages that leaders go through that can't be skipped – no more than a baby learns to run before it crawls. At each stage the entrepreneur builds on the strengths of previous stages which means it is likely that you will see elements of yourself in several of the stages. Just because you pass through one stage to the next, unlike other progressions, you do not 'leave the previous level behind'; rather like an oil painting you build up the layers one on another, all remaining present but creating a newer picture.

First of all give yourself an honest appraisal of what type of Entrepreneur that you are currently, see Table 1.

While it is likely that you'll see elements of your style of business leadership in many of the stages, typically there is a "centre of gravity". In other words one of the stages has the most pull. At the bottom of the table the thinking and leading styles are increasingly complex. These stages take

Stage	Characteristics
Opportunistic	Wins any way possible. Good in emergencies.
Diplomat	Avoids conflict. Brings people together.
Expert	Rules by expertise. Good as a sole trader.
Achiever	Effectively achieves through teams. Good at managing.
Individualist	Self in relationship to system. Invents new rules, provides consultancy.
Strategist	Achieves balance between short and long term. Transformational leader.
Alchemist	Integrates, material, spiritual and societal transformation. Society wide transformations.

Table 1 (Rooke & Torbert, 2005)

information from multiple sources and consider decisions from multiple perspectives – less than 1% of the population are reported to have achieved this stage.

Once you recognise where you are, the focus for your growth is developing your skills in that stage and the one above. All that really means is that the growing edge for people is different. To use a tennis analogy, some people will need to work on their forehand and others their serve. Typically the serve isn't practised until at least rudimentary racket and ball control is achieved.

Most of the successful entrepreneurs I have met are at the Expert stage or beyond. Indeed many businesses are started by experts in a particular aspect of their business. For example, engineers start engineering businesses, builders start building companies, IT specialists start IT businesses ... you get the idea. The growing edge for the Expert is developing from being quite literally the expert, through to achieving their business objectives through other people.

> Simon had been a builder, and several years ago started a construction company. In order for him to grow beyond a very small business (1 – 3-man) he needed an office team. He doesn't do much building these days – he's had to learn a whole range of new skills, from embracing the finances as well as developing the skills of managing others – not just the tradesmen, but also his office team – as well as liaising with clients.

When a business owner first starts to manage and empower others, it can feel like they're relinquishing power. All transitions between the stages can feel hard, they take you out of your comfort zone – a sure indicator that you're growing. You're leaving behind what you know and have competence in, and are starting a new phase of growth.

> Originally Simon was involved in everything to do with his business, he knew all the answers. As his business grew, and he began to work longer and longer – he realised he had to relinquish some control to his team. Of course he needed systems to track and monitor workflows – but he had become the bottleneck to growing his business.

Although growth between stages happens naturally, the catalyst is often some type of event that causes you to take a step back and see things more objectively. I've seen the stimulus for change coming from different aspects of business.

For example: from landing a significant new order, expanding the team, through to the recognition that there's a real problem with managing cash flow. One company lost a significant bid that they expected to win – which caused them to examine their processes to see how they could improve and avoid losing another.

Growth requires the entrepreneur to spend time working 'on' their business rather than 'in' their business. Because entrepreneurs are often so busy engaged with the day to day running of their business, for most business owners this more strategic focus doesn't happen as often as it could. Growth requires some type of change.

Some people think they're 'too long in the tooth' to change. Remembering Ford's quote at the beginning of this chapter – it could be that just your thoughts about whether or not you can change either keeps you stuck or growing.

Science (both neurologically and psychologically) has proven that there is no physical reason why you can't learn new skills and attitudes at any time during your life. Often it is fear that is at the root. Fear of change, or fear of failure.

The speed of change
The good news is that sometimes change can be instantaneous. When change is this quick, often new

information is the cause of the change. There's the old joke about the ship and the lighthouse – I've just spoilt the punch line. The commander of the ship radios the other vessel, not realising it's a lighthouse, requesting it divert its course. The lower ranked officer from the lighthouse recommends they divert their course. The commander gets annoyed and tries to pull rank, both with his status and the status of the ship – until the lower ranking officer points out that they're a lighthouse.

Although it's a joke, it does a great job of demonstrating how quickly a "U" turn can be made when you're open to hearing new information – and not just in emergency situations.

Develop your mindset
There are two different mindsets, fixed and growth, which produce very different results.

A quick test: consider your views on intelligence. Do you believe intelligence is a fixed trait that can't be changed? Or do you believe it's a more malleable part of a person's make-up?

When a person holds a fixed mindset about an aspect of themselves or another person, they believe that traits such as intelligence are fixed and can't be changed. The growth mindset has been shown to be more effective in producing better results. With a growth mindset comes a willingness to learn. A growth mindset often supports and enables effort, persistence and dedication, with which you can change almost every aspect of yourself – if you so wish.

The fixed mindset
When someone has a fixed mindset about something it means

that they don't willingly engage in the new activity, they don't pursue learning, and therefore their results become self-fulfilling: they get what they expect! They don't believe they can do something, and without effort, experiencing the odd failure and learning from it … guess what – they don't learn to do something different.

Generally a fixed mindset is related to someone who believes they already know the answers, and therefore don't need to be open to new information. It can also be related to someone who believes they can't learn anything new.

> For example, occasionally I get a client who has their head in the sand about a particular aspect of their business, typically either sales or finances. They feel that they 'should' know more, they often don't know what help they need, which makes it harder to ask for the necessary assistance to understand the language of numbers.

It's probably a useful aside to mention that the *person* isn't 'fixed'; it's merely an 'attitude' that becomes fixed. Attitudes are held about a particular area of one's life – and of course attitudes can and do change.

I've noticed that sometimes success can cause people to fix their mindset, to plateau or even to stagnate. It seems that achieving success causes people to become slightly entrenched and less open to new information. Perhaps it's because they think "this way worked before, it should work again". It's only by setting new and higher goals that the change process can really begin. When your responses become too automatic it closes down your ability to see new opportunities.

Alex was successful in retail and had created an out-of-town independent warehouse which for several years had successfully attracted shoppers from a large catchment area. However, he began to realise that more and more people wanted to order online. His business was not set up for the online world. He railed against it (the fixed mindset), as the whole online world was new to him.

If you notice yourself responding with "yeah, yeah, I know", or "not interested" – based on very little evidence – you're closing down to new information. Alternatively perhaps in hindsight you noticed that something had caused you to become defensive – these are pretty good indicators of a fixed mindset. Or you may notice your body telling you what you are subconsciously thinking, i.e., crossing your arms, a frown on your face.

The growth mindset

It's scientifically proven that the growth mindset is more effective in producing better results (Dweck, 2006). With a growth mindset comes a willingness to learn.

You've probably got more of a growth mindset in situations where you notice that you're curious for more information, where you ask questions. You may also notice yourself making the odd mistake, and depending on the context you might find you can gently laugh at yourself, and delight in finding new ways of doing things or discovering novel ideas and approaches that stop you in your mental tracks.

So that you can deliberately adopt the growth mindset, next

time you notice that you have a growth mindset, take a moment to note how you feel. What thoughts run through your mind? What's your posture like? What words or phrases do you regularly hear yourself say, either to yourself or others?

> As Alex started to explore technology he became increasingly curious about how it could be harnessed for his business. He had a clear goal – and the technology became a mechanism for achieving his goal.

A growth mindset also means you're more likely to persevere through both the frustrations and excitement of learning. In the depth of that frustration, at conscious incompetence, it's even more important to have the ability to maintain the growth mindset – or switch into it as soon as you notice language of self-doubt creeping in: "I can't do this, it's too hard; I should never have started this …"

Perhaps as a business owner you can relate to the experience of employing your first team member.

> Prior to his first employee starting, Ian was exhilarated; he had hopes and expectations that his workload would reduce. This euphoria was quickly dampened by the realisation that his new employee needed training, needed his time (which he felt he didn't have), and that the systems in place that worked for Ian were not sufficient for two people. Ian had to invest time and further develop his processes so that work would not 'fall between the gap' of two people. A growth mindset meant that Ian was able to persevere through this experience.

Which mindset are you using?

Neither the fixed nor the growth mindset is right or wrong, although for advancement and business growth, not to mention having an interesting and varied life, a growth mindset will prove more advantageous. However, business success is more likely to occur in areas where a growth mindset is adopted because you're more likely to do new things – to learn from them – to see new opportunities and take action.

It's likely that you have different mindsets in different areas of your life. Think about the skills in a range of areas, for example, juggling, playing golf, singing, business, legal issues, IT, accounting. There are probably many areas that you are open to learning. "Sure, I'll take some legal advice." Whereas, there will be other areas where a fixed mindset will kick in: "Sing? Me? Never!" It's useful to be aware of a situation where you use a growth mindset and a fixed mindset. Knowing you use both, you can then begin to change into the growth mindset at will.

Start by taking note of which mindset you're operating in which environment. Notice the attributes of both, so that you can start to consciously adjust to the growth mindset, and be open to new learning and new opportunities in any situation.

Developing the awareness that's required to notice your mindset moment by moment takes practice. To ease into it gently I recommend you take five minutes towards the end of your work day. Reflect on the day that's taken place, and the evening before. Jot down the key activities that you were involved with and take a moment to remember whether they caused you to become a bit closed and defensive (signs of the fixed mindset), or whether you were open, curious and questioning (indicators of the growth mindset).

Developing your growth mindset

Opportunities are available to us all – so why is it that sometimes only relatively few people see them? I believe it's because some people just see the world differently, and maintaining a growth mindset is one way that you can see the world differently, and be alert to the opportunities.

Look at the picture. What do you see?

A white vase, or two faces looking at each other? Both are there. I think the same is often true in life, opportunities and problems are all around us. This section has been about developing the mental flexibility to be open to see opportunities. When you look at a situation you can ask yourself, and others: what's new about this situation? What can I learn from it? Where's the opportunity? This is very different from a more closed, fixed mindset response of: "I've seen this before; just like the last one." This categorising of situations as "the same" can enable you to operate on automatic pilot, but it also means that you might miss nuances and opportunities which arise from slight differences.

Using the analogy of a holiday: you are an experienced traveller, you probably know the type of things to pack and you're worldly wise. Remember the destination is new – keep an open mind to spot and navigate past the obstacles and to find opportunities for adventure, which are often nestling in obscure corners.

> TIP: One of the quickest ways to change your mindset is to change some of the environmental factors, the people you hang out with, and the books you read. One of my mentors described it this way: "Good books and good company stop the weeds from growing in your mind."

A key step in achieving greater success is defining your vision – creating a compelling new vision. It means being open to and seeking change and perhaps some risk too. This is where having a growth mindset pays dividends.

The learning edge

In our instant gratification society I've noticed that if something is not easy, many people quit too soon with their learning. Therefore knowing **how** you learn means that you can develop the business edge faster by knowing how to persevere longer. Learning anything can take patience – often entrepreneurs want quick results. Learning can take time and at times can be frustrating – but the benefits of persevering with learning will give you the edge in business.

Most people think you either know something or you don't, that it's a black and white approach, something is either learned or not – but learning is a process, starting with something being outside our awareness. Typically as we become more aware of our lack of skills, frustration kicks in – and often this is where people quit learning and revert back to their old ways. Slowly skills are developed, and typically use full concentration. Remember when you were first learning how to drive – it took your full conscious attention, whereas now you probably jump in the car and drive without thinking.

For many skills you need as a business owner it's not necessary to get to the automatic stage. There may be some things that always seem to remain a deliberate focussed effort – for many owners it can be the focus on their profitability.

By understanding that learning is a process can help you to stay engaged with the learning. Remember that these stages of learning apply equally to your team and to you, to both skills and mindset development. As a leader you'll give people on your team different types of support when their skills and confidence are at different stages.

> Within one small company Gordon, an employee, knew how to do his job, and therefore was promoted to tele-sales team-leader. Whilst Gordon knew how to make calls and remain self-motivated, he didn't initially have the skills to support his team. In the early stages of taking on his new role, he needed more support and encouragement than he had previously – as well as a bit more "how to" information. Being needed for additional support initially came as a surprise to the business owner – who expected that Gordon would be ultra-productive with his new responsibilities from day one.

You too may need different support at different stages, otherwise there is a risk that you quit (learning, retreat and retrench). How many business owners have you come across that grew their business, only to find running a team too hard, so they went back to doing it alone? Consider who can provide you with that level of support.

As you begin developing your entrepreneurial mindset, you may experience moments of heightened awareness, and frustration that your mindset isn't fully supporting you to achieve your goals. This experience is ***normal***. Whilst feeling the frustration – congratulate yourself for learning something new and remember the process of learning!

Create your vision
As you consider the vision for your company, think specifically what's your role in the business but also include your personal vision, and some personal goals – fun, holidays and things that you do to re-energise yourself. Some people are really clear on their vision, and that's great, but many people have 'lost' their vision in the stress of running their business. I've found that typically different people need a different stimulus for thinking about their vision.

For example (figure 1), some people can start with some big or lifetime goals. Others want to design a life whereby they do more of what they enjoy. Some people find it useful to project themselves forward and look back – depending on your mental wiring you could put yourself in a beautiful celebration of your 80th birthday, listening to speeches from friends, family and former business associates and employees about your achievements. Alternatively some people find motivation from writing their obituary, assuming that they make no changes to their life. Whilst this in itself doesn't provide a vision, it normally provides a boost of energy to do *something* different! Knowing what's important to you, your values can also be a source of information about what else you can do.

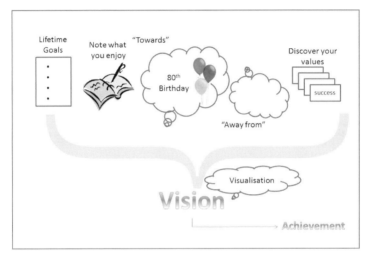

Figure 1

Think long term about the full range of areas of your life, from finances and the monthly income you want or need for the lifestyle that you want. Think about hobbies, family, friends, holidays, community.

I've noticed one thing that can stop people in setting their vision is that they don't know how to achieve it. The vision comes first, the plan comes second – keep them separate at the vision creation stage. This is worth repeating. Be sure to separate creating your vision and planning how to get there.

Alex had developed a strong vision. I believe that this, in part, was why he was able to be open-minded and explore technology. Simon had a stonking goal to build his business – which I think gave him the determination to succeed in learning other aspects of business.

Having a vision for your business forms the foundation for goal setting, and is fundamental to long term success. In the words of George Harrison, "If you don't know where you're going, any road will take you there." Many people I coach don't like the idea of goal setting, they feel it detracts from their ability to be flexible. However, I've noticed that people who have a long term vision, and who have goals, also know what their priorities are – and they are more likely to stay focussed and committed to their priorities. If you know what your priorities are, you're more likely to know if something is an opportunity or if it's a bit of a distraction. You remain flexible, but have a "yardstick" to measure the new against.

Goals

On one hand it seems easy: say what you're going to do (the goal), and do it. But in practice it seems that for most people consistently achieving goals is a little more complex. You may have come across the term SMART goals. It's the commonly used acronym for goal setting. Goals should be Specific, Measureable, Achievable, Realistic and Timebound. If you use this approach and it works for you – great – skip this section. I've found for many people, whilst even if they can recite the words – they don't put it into practice. I've found an adaptation works.

What follows are some simple, effective and proven tips for

achieving success. You don't have to memorise them. Write it down, put it on your phone, stick it on your wall, and set your goals with these criteria.

Vision: Check how the goal fits with your vision. Assuming that the vision is something you want, achieving the goal should be motivating. If it's not, check whether **you** have to do the task – could someone else do it?

Size: There are different size goals for different time periods. For example your 5 – 10-year vision should be a stretch goal and it should be challenging. Whereas your 90-day goal should be achievable and realistic, and daily goals or tasks should be so small that it becomes a "no-brainer" to do them.

Underwhelming: Not all goals are fab and fun, there may be important things that only you can do. For these goals, make progress little and often. Divide goals, especially challenging ones, into really small pieces. Only do what you set out to do – make it easy for yourself to have a mini success each time you work at it. Achieving success will make it easier to resume the task the next time.

Cross-off-able: One way you can check if a goal is specific is to ask yourself: "When it's done, will I be able to cross it off the list?" One common mistake is that people have goals that are nebulous and vague. Whilst this may be easy to write down – it's far harder to complete.

> Ian had a nebulous goal of "maintain social media presence". He noticed that it never was complete, so he changed it to "tweet once per day, blog weekly".

Get strategic – make progress

You might have noticed that "stuff to do" typically falls into one of two categories. There are things to do to keep your business moving forward day to day. This is described as working 'in' your business. There is also more strategic, longer term planning – often described as working 'on' your business. Essentially the entrepreneur has to work more 'on' their business than 'in' it, and for most people this transition is not an overnight process, although it is probably the single most important transition a business owner must complete.

As you look at Table 1 of types of business leader, you will notice that there are some general things that change with leaders at a more advanced level. Communication skills increase as there is usually a broader range of people to communicate with. Another example is increasing levels of trust – from doing tasks yourself to trusting others to do them, and having workflow systems in place. As the day-to-day work is no longer done by the founder, by necessity systems and communication skills have to increase so that information is passed around the organisation effectively.

As an entrepreneur you certainly have the ability to see opportunities that others haven't – that's why you started your business. But as the business grows, often you can become so immersed that you don't have time to see new opportunities. So here are a couple of ideas to get you to begin to think differently and ultimately more strategically.

Flick the switches

I'm going to suggest you swap things around. Imagine a switch with "automatic" and "pay attention". The things that you do automatically – start to pay more attention to, and some of the tasks that you're giving conscious thought to – automate.

Automate these things

There will be things that you spend time deliberating. For example, what to do next, when to make the call to the client, when to check for email (again) – or even respond as you notice the new alert. Don't use your prime thinking capacity on insignificant decisions. These are the things that you need to automate, or have a process in place as much as possible. Don't waste your thinking on "shall I make calls first or check email".

These low value activities, that you currently spend time thinking about – automate. Make a plan, take out the constant decision making but set aside time to respond – these constant little decisions sap energy. It seems that we have a capacity for decision making, but that capacity gets used up with insignificant decisions.

When I first met Ian, a business owner of a professional services company, his personal time management was what was holding him back. One of the first things he did was to create a "default diary" to begin to automate some of his routine work.

Pay attention to these things

Another way to describe automatic is unconscious competence. For the things you do automatically, flick the switch and do them with more conscious awareness (conscious competence).

For example your thoughts occur, but most people don't explore what's going on – whether thoughts are useful or self-sabotaging. In order to further develop your winning mindset – I suggest for at least part of the day you "pay attention" to your thoughts, notice whether you're approaching a situation from either a growth or a fixed mindset.

Focus your time doing tasks effectively. This will give you more thinking and decision making capacity to focus on the strategic activities, as well as creative energy to focus on innovations. Make a conscious decision to take a step back and notice additional tasks which you'd be better to delegate, outsource or hire someone to do. Create a perpetual action list, or a default diary to release your mental capacity.

More switches

Creativity occurs in two contrasting situations: desperation and happiness. You've probably heard the quote "necessity is the mother of invention". When people are up against it, with clear limits on their creativity – often solutions "just come to mind". I don't wish those "back against the wall" type situations upon you. You'll therefore be pleased to know that creativity also happens when things are going well and people are feeling positive.

Many people go into business to get more control – they feel that it will be more enjoyable. But somewhere along the line, for some business people I meet, the enjoyment has dissipated into the ether. We have the power to choose. Even in dire circumstances of concentration camps of the second world war, Frankl (2004) noted, *"Everything can be taken from a man but one thing: the last of the human freedoms – to choose one's attitude in any given set of circumstances, to choose one's own way."*

Emotions are not passive things that happen to us. We can be proactive in switching our emotions and there's enormous benefit in doing so.

It would be easy to overlook positive emotions perhaps because many people do not really understand them and therefore see them as irrelevant for business. However, they're important in so many aspects of business that I have devoted the final section to them. Next I give seven reasons that positive emotions are important for you and your business.

Positive emotions to supercharge your business for greater success

For many years the overwhelming opinion was that being successful *led to* happiness. It seems logical to think that it's easier for someone to be happy *after* they've made their fortune. However, research from the field of positive psychology has demonstrated that ***positive emotions actually lead to success***. Happier people naturally attract more opportunities and are in a better frame of mind to make more of these opportunities. Therefore happiness *leads to* success. There's even a scientifically proven ratio for the proportion of positive emotions to the number of negative emotions which, once reached, shows a positive impact on health, well-being and success. Positive emotions range in energy from high energy (e.g., jumping for joy) to lower energy feelings of contentment, and the good news is that they all count as positive emotions, although some are clearly more appropriate than others in any given situation.

Besides leading to success, here are seven more reasons why you should set time aside to focus on feeling good.

Health: Positive emotions are good for your health, they increase the number of antibodies – essential for fighting infection and keeping fit. It's easier to do your best work when you're feeling healthy.

Broaden thinking – noticing opportunities: Some emotions protect us from danger, but narrow the range of immediate options for action: "fight or flight". Conversely positive emotions *broaden* our outlook, and we notice more opportunities. My recommendation then is to actively find things to be positive about. Aim to filter the news – or stop watching it altogether – you can use the internet to get really specific about the information you seek. Notice your mood and seek to do more of the activities you find uplifting and you will attract more positive interactions.

Opportunity magnet: In addition to noticing opportunities, you will also become a magnet for others giving you opportunities. Be the person that radiates good emotions – you will attract other like-minded people and you will more likely be the person they think of when there's an opportunity.

Builds resilience: Resilience is the ability to "power through" tougher times without experiencing detrimental effects on mental or physical health. It gives you staying power when the going gets tough.

Create positive memories: When you experience positive emotions or experiences. Take time to remember them, take time to savour them. Research has shown that people who actively take time to remember good times, are mindful in the moment and who have goals, enjoy life more, and live longer.

Moods go viral: The feel good factor is contagious – spread it within your team! "Catch people doing something well", and offer a word of praise, a smile, or a genuine compliment. Your team members will experience all the benefits of positive emotions – and don't be surprised if they go the extra distance to help someone on the team, or your prospects or customers.

Build high performing teams: Encourage positive emotions on your team. It takes between three and eleven positive emotions to counter each negative emotion. A positive team is more creative, sees more opportunities and is more successful.

So, to supercharge your business, get a daily dose of positive emotions!

Action plan for developing positive emotions

The first thing to recognise is that sometimes we all get stuck in a mood; snapping out of a mood is not always easy, and getting frustrated with yourself won't help.

The second step is to develop your 'mood lifting' plan. The best time to develop this plan is when you're feeling up-beat. It contains some of the following elements:

1. Stay calm, breathe more deeply (see below)

2. Develop and use your plan:

    a. Listen to uplifting music
    b. Remind yourself of good times by looking at some photos
    c. Physical activity (e.g., a walk)

3. Develop and use your sense of perspective

The third step is to use the plan when you notice yourself slipping into a bad mood – to help jump-start yourself into a better mood. If it's appropriate, then make the decision to JUMP right out of it into a positive mood.

This chapter has provided some tips that you can implement immediately. Remember to engage your growth mindset. If positive emotions are not what you've done before, you may feel a bit uncomfortable; don't worry, that's a good thing. It's a sign that you've stepped outside your comfort zone – and are growing!

Alan says:

This book is asking you the entrepreneur to think in different ways than you might have been on a regular basis before in order for you to take advantage of the opportunities which undoubtedly lie ahead for your company.

This chapter, written by someone who has plenty of experience of getting into entrepreneurs' brains, shows that it is perfectly possible that, if you so wish, you can change your level of acceptance of new learning without having to ditch any of your own received wisdom. In fact you can use it as a plank to launch yourself into a whole new growth mindset and overcome with enthusiasm the frustrations of taking on new approaches in driving your business to a new level of performance.

SOURCES OF FINANCE TO GROW YOUR BUSINESS

Peter Kelly

Banks are not the only sources of funds and may not even be the best source for your needs.

Peter Kelly lets you in on access to multiple sources of finance

It is interesting to note that the traditional source of finance, the major high street banks, are complaining that they are not getting enough demand from small to medium sized companies for the money that they have available to lend. The SMEs on the other hand are telling a different story and are complaining that the banks are just not lending. It is a confusing situation and as always there is some truth in both sides of the argument. The banks have been told to improve their liquidity and their balance sheets and not to take risks, while at the same time they are being told to lend more money to get the economy growing again. It is a very difficult juggling act for them to satisfy these conflicting government demands. The recent facts and figures announced concerning the Merlin agreement indicate that the overall lending by the banks exceeded the government's target, and that £8 billion more was lent to SMEs in the last 12 months than was lent in the previous 12 months. Yet still the SME lending target was missed by £1 billion, so the banks must do better. But at the same time SMEs put on deposit in the banks more money than they have done for the last 20 years. So over the last 12 months it looks as if the banks have been lending more, but not enough to satisfy the government, while at the same time many businesses have decided not to take risks and to conserve their capital until things start to improve. This is also shown by the fact that during 2011 the proportion of SMEs using external finance declined and this was especially marked in SMEs of fewer than 10 employees (SME Finance Monitor, Q4 2011). This seems to be backed up by a recent Deloitte report, which indicates that British companies are hoarding cash because of economic uncertainty. This research shows that companies are holding £64 billion more working capital than they need to fund day-to-day operations. If released it could be used to expand businesses or smooth downturns in the market.

An important question, therefore, is what are companies planning to do over the next three months and how does that differ from the previous 12 months? The SME Finance monitor, compiled by BDRC, throws out some interesting facts. Their findings are based on more than 15,000 telephone interviews conducted among businesses with a turnover of up to £25m between February and December 2011.

The most important finding was that 14% of SMEs are planning to apply for finance in the near future. At the same time they discovered that in the last quarter of 2011 fewer companies applied for new or renewed overdraft facilities than in Q1-2 of 2011 and there was also a decline in loan applications. The overall figure for applications for new and renewed facilities stands at 9% for Q4 compared to 15% in Q1-2. So the banks are correct in saying that last year they were getting fewer applications.

It is also interesting to note from the monitor that there were signs of improvement in terms of the number of loans being approved. While applications made in Q4 2010 or Q1 2011 were less likely to succeed, there was an improvement in Q2 2011 that was partially maintained in Q3. Overdraft success rates were at 79% and loan success rates stood at 63%. Automatic renewal of overdrafts increased overdraft success rates to a staggering level of 93% in Q4. Another revelation in the monitor shows that over the last 12 months 78% of SMEs neither applied for finance nor wanted it. This was up from the 68% in Q1-2 2011.

This improvement in access to finance seems to be continuing. The second quarter of 2012 has already seen some improvement in credit conditions for Britain's manufacturers, according to a major survey published by EEF. The Q2 Credit Conditions Survey has shown that the availability of finance increased for more companies during the past two months, albeit at a higher cost. This survey has shown improvements across several measures of the availability of finance. A stronger balance of companies (4.3%) reported availability of new lines of borrowing during the last two months and, encouragingly, a positive balance of companies (+1%) reported improved availability of credit on existing arrangements, the first time there has been a positive balance since Q3 2007. But the balance of companies reporting an increase in the overall cost of credit still remains firmly in negative territory and has worsened since Q1 of this year, to 21.2%. This appears to be driven by fees and other costs of lending, with a higher balance of companies (16.2%) reporting higher fees on existing borrowing.

The picture is still very confused; it is true that bank lending to

SMEs by the end of 2012 will shrink by 4.6%, dropping by £430bn, but the rate of decline is slower than in 2011, when lending dropped by 6.1%. Let us hope that this is the last year of such declines, but be warned that many economists predict that bank lending will not recover to the levels of 2008 for another 4 years, 2016, and naturally the SMEs will bear the brunt of it.

My own experience has shown that the banks are willing to lend money to good companies, with strong balance sheets, that are profitable, where the directors accept the need for personal guarantees and where there is a specific reason for the loan that will enable the company to grow. General working capital and cash flow needs are not normally reasons for lending. There is no money for those companies that are not making money, with negative balance sheets, no appetite for personal guarantees, and who already have arrears with HMRC. The problem is, however, that the world is not just made up of good and bad companies. There is a layer of companies that are neither good nor bad; those sit in the middle and are finding it hard to raise the growth capital that they need.

It seems clear, therefore, that some banks are lending more money than previously (and that others are not) and that SMEs, having gone through a phase of consolidation, are beginning to look for additional capital to grow their business. If you fall into the category that the banks will lend to then you are fortunate, but if you fall into the middle layer of not quite being good enough yet, where do you go for the growth funding that you need?

The first thing to understand is not to rush into anything and to make careful preparations before applying for any type of funding at all. Complete a credit check on your own company; find out what the funding providers will see about your company. Make certain that County Court Judgements, if any, are satisfied before you apply. Check that any debentures that other funders may hold are still applicable and if not have these removed. It is shocking how many funding providers and managing directors fail to remove all expired asset debentures from the records. Also make certain that you are up to date with filing your latest set of accounts.

It really does not matter what type of funding you require, most providers will want the same information from you; have it prepared in advance. The information that will be required is:

- Prepare a detailed business plan with forecasts for at least the next 12 months and a solid explanation of what the funds will be used for and why your company is safe to lend to. All sales and financial assumptions must be explained in full.

- Your last filed accounts.

- Your latest management accounts. If you do not normally produce management accounts then start to do them. Lenders do not like companies that do not have sight of what is happening to their financial wellbeing on a monthly basis. But do not just produce monthly management figures, have monthly management meetings to discuss the figures as well. This helps to create a greater feeling of responsibility amongst the whole management team and gives them good insights into the challenges faced by other departments.

- Aged debtors and aged creditors. These show a snapshot of whether the company owes more money than they are owed and how well the management team are managing their cash flow.

- Discuss in advance with all the directors their willingness and ability to provide personal guarantees. It is unrealistic in today's market place to expect funders to provide loans if the directors are not prepared to support their own company.

- It is also useful to prepare a document outlining how the company has been funded in the past and a list of all borrowings that are still current. A record of the directors' personal investment in the company is also very useful, to prove commitment.

- Make certain that you are up front about any past skeletons that may be in the cupboard, such as past liquidations or County Court Judgements, and have a detailed explanation as to why these occurred and what actions you took to remedy the situation. Funding providers do not like discovering these skeletons themselves and prefer the funding applicant to provide full disclosure in the first place. It should also be noted that if a bank or other funding provider lost money in a past liquidation then the likelihood of a new provider offering further funds is limited.

I have just had a case where a company was refused funding because the managing director's brother had a recent liquidation in his past and he was now working for his brother, my client. Because this was not disclosed by the brothers at the beginning of the funding application, it went badly for them at the credit committee stage.

Once you are prepared you can now start approaching the relevant providers. Always do this in a parallel fashion approaching a few at the same time. Do not do it one at a time, waiting to fail with one until you move to the next. A prospect of mine had been using the serial method for 9 months before he asked me to help and because of the 9 month time delay his position had become more difficult and he had lost valuable orders that could not be fulfilled because of cash flow difficulties. Create competition amongst the providers; after all they are just like any other sales organisation, they are just selling money rather than another type of product. It is also advisable to get specialist help when looking for funding. This can normally be done on a 'success only' fee basis and their knowledge of the market place and the individuals concerned can be invaluable and can save you and your management team a great deal of time. One client of mine had been turned down by a major high street bank and had given up on that bank completely. I knew a very creative manager in a different branch of the same bank and the loan application was approved with little trouble.

The most logical place for you to go for funding is your own bank. You have a history with them and they should understand your business better than a new provider. If they are willing to help you then the normal types of funding that they should provide are:

- Overdraft facilities
- Commercial loans, including the EFG and the new NLGS schemes
- Commercial mortgages
- Invoice discounting or factoring
- Trade finance for both imports and exports
- Asset finance for plant and machinery and vehicles
- Foreign exchange services
- Treasury solutions

If, however, your own bank will not provide funding for you then you should seriously consider a total re-banking exercise. Resent research from the OFT, Research Now and Mintel shows that the percentage of companies switching banks between 2000 and 2006 increased to 13% and those that have switched or had considered switching had reached 39%. If your company is strong then you most probably will not need to consider switching, but if you are in that difficult layer between strong and weak then this is an option to be taken seriously. It is an unfortunate fact of life that new clients are often treated better than existing ones. When thinking about switching banks, think out of the box and do not just consider the main high street banks but also consider banks such as Metro, Clydesdale, Handlesbanken, Bank of Cyprus and Bank of China.

If you cannot get support from your bank, and even if you can, it is often better not to put all your financial eggs in one basket. Always consider using some of the many independent providers that are able to provide you with alternative funding options. The independents can offer you the following funding solutions:

- Invoice discounting or factoring
- Trade finance
- Asset finance, both new and sale and lease back
- Angel funding, both equity and debt
- Turnaround finance
- Crowdfunding

I would like to consider, in more detail, each of these independent sources of finance.

Invoice Discounting or Factoring

This is one of the easiest forms of finance to obtain but is often misunderstood. In basic terms you are selling your invoices to a provider the day you issue them and therefore not having to wait up to 60+ days to get paid by your clients. It is normally better to go to one of the many independent providers as they are smaller, more flexible and you are individually much more important to them, a larger fish in a smaller pond.

There are some very interesting new developments in this market place. Traditionally you were often asked to sign an agreement for up to three years and sometimes with an additional six months cancellation clause on top. Providers would also insist on you having to give them the full debtor ledger, even those that paid in 7-10 days. Nowadays you can negotiate rolling monthly contracts and there is even one company offering a rolling weekly contract. No need to tie yourself to long term contracts that you might not need in the future. In my opinion a 12 month contract with a three month cancellation clause is a happy medium. Another interesting new development has been the introduction of single invoice discounting facilities. These providers are happy to only provide funds against a single or a handful of invoices on an occasional basis. No fixed term contract at all. Many companies find this type of funding very useful when corporation tax or VAT due dates come around. It is also a good method of funding an unexpected large order that otherwise you may have to turn down. For single invoice discounting, however, you do have to overcome one hurdle, your own bank. If you have an overdraft it is very likely that your bank will hold an all asset debenture over your company and they must be persuaded to give up this security over the invoices you want to sell. Some, not all, banks make this difficult for you. One of my clients had given up looking for this type of finance because of his bank's refusal to give up their security. I took up his case and found a single invoice discounter who was prepared to take a second charge over the assets and so not diminish the incumbent bank's security.

There are also some bad new trends that have come into this industry. The first is that the directors will now always be asked to give personal guarantees. The trick here is to negotiate the level of these guarantees. The providers already have the security of the invoices and should be quite happy with only a small level of directors' guarantees. You should agree to no more than 10-20% of the total facility level. It is the provider's way of making certain the directors stay around if the company fails, so that the people who know the clients best will help them to collect any outstanding payments.

You must also be very careful of minimum base rate clauses. Some organisations are quoting the Bank of England base rate as their base rate. All well and good until you see in the very small print a clause, which states that there is a minimum base rate of 3%. This will mean that you are paying 2.5% more than you actually thought.

It is very easy for you to arrange a bad invoice discounting or factoring agreement for yourself. This minimum base rate clause is just one example. Remember everything is negotiable. Concentration levels are another area that you have to be careful of. Most providers will originally limit you to a concentration level of around 25%. This means that if a single client accounts for more than 40% of your monthly turnover then you will not be allowed to put the last 15% through the facility and therefore will raise less money than you thought. On top of not raising as much money as they thought, one client of mine found that they were also paying the full service charge on the same invoices that were being refused funding. The providers of this sort of finance will also exclude from the agreement any of your clients that they believe pose too much of a risk. Remember that exclusions should be a two way street. Before you sign any agreement make certain that you have excluded all your clients who pay quickly, you do not need to finance these. Just like any other sales organisation, a funding salesman will negotiate with you before you have signed the agreement. After you have signed it is much more difficult.

It is important to plan ahead; for example will you want trade finance in the future or even an EFG loan and will you start exporting? If any of these are likely then make certain that you carry out your invoice discounting with a company that provides all these services as well.

One company that I was dealing with knew in advance that it would need a loan, within two years, of £50,000 to move to new premises. Their bank had already turned them down for loans in the past. When finding the right independent provider of invoice discounting for them I kept this requirement in mind and arranged a facility with a company that would offer them an over payment on their invoice discounting facility that would act as a loan. Another client knew that they would want a loan for future expansion and so when it came to their invoice discounting requirement I arranged it with one of the few providers that also offered Enterprise Finance Guarantee Scheme loans to their existing clients. In both these cases, if these future requirements were not thought about in advance then they would have had to go through the pain and expense of switching invoice discounting providers, which if you have signed a three year agreement can be very costly.

Trade and stock finance

Trade and stock finance are quite similar in nature. Trade finance is the funding of imports, and also locally sourced goods and sometimes components, for which you are already holding firm orders from creditworthy clients. Stock finance is the funding of goods or components just for stock and where there are no firm orders to hand. Stock finance is one of the most difficult forms of funding to find.

The first point of call for trade or stock finance is normally your own bank, but if that is not an option there are other sources available. Most funders of this type will insist that the trade finance is linked to their own Invoice discounting or factoring facilities, so that they control both sides of the transaction and thereby reduce their risk. It is natural, therefore, that after the banks the next people to approach are the invoice discounting and factoring providers. There are three or four that also offer trade finance. If you are already tied into a provider that does not offer trade finance, then you need to consider if it is worthwhile changing to one that does; this will involve cost, or you can approach one of the very few organisations that offer standalone trade finance. They will also need to link it to a third party invoice discounting or factoring facility, but it does not have to be their own. Trade finance is not cheap but you need to think about it as just another cost of sale; without it you may not be able to fulfil the order at all. Most providers charge by the month and part thereof, so one month and a few days equates to two months charges; so the longer the payment terms that you can negotiate with the manufacturer the better.

A good example of this was a client of mine who imported from China, but had to pay for the shipment in full before the goods could be shipped. The Chinese company would not give any credit at all to this small organisation. This meant that my client either had to find the funds from already tight cash flow, or try to borrow the funds from expensive lenders for up to three months. The answer was to find a trade finance company that would issue a letter of credit to the Chinese, who were then happy to ship the goods without payment, except for a small deposit, because the letter of credit was issued by an organisation that had financial strength. Full payment was then made on presentation of the bills of lading. At this point an import loan was made to my client, to cover the price of the goods. The goods were then delivered to the end user, my client issued an invoice, which was paid with 24 hours by an invoice discounter and the import loan was paid off within a few days. The result was that my client only borrowed the cost of the shipment for less than a week rather than for three or four months, not only saving money but also not impacting his already tight cash flow.

Stock finance is also charged by the month or part thereof and some of the providers will insist that the stock is kept in their own warehouses until it is called off and paid for. Funders always have to think the worst and how they will get their money back if the client defaults, so the stock must have a ready market at a reasonable and profitable price, just in case they get left holding it. Credit insurance is normally taken out covering the company that wants the funding, so the amount of stock funding offered is linked to the credit insurance available.

Asset finance, both new and sale and lease back

Hire Purchase, also known as lease purchase, allows you to spread the full cost of an asset over a defined period. At the end of that period, provided you stick to the terms of the agreement, you will own the asset. Capital allowances may be available as a deduction against your tax bill. If your business is registered for VAT you can also claim back the VAT on the asset up front. Also any interest that you pay can be offset against profits.

Leasing: Although a finance lease will look and feel the same as a hire purchase, you will not end up owning the asset at the end of the contract. Ownership remains with the finance company at all times. At the end of the period you are usually offered a new term at a nominal fee.

Leasing can be arranged from terms as short as six months

up to five years and more. Most asset types can be leased, from plant and machinery and vehicles, to IT equipment, including computers, servers, printers, telecoms and even some software.

Most Hire Purchase and Leasing companies will want to make certain that they are taking as little risk as possible with their funds. They will, therefore, want to make certain that the company requesting finance is well funded, profitable and with a positive balance sheet. At least one of the directors must own a property in the UK and they will want to be able to see that the company can afford the monthly payments. Personal guarantees from the directors are usually required. It is possible to obtain leasing and HP for start-up organisations but personal guarantees will always be asked for and the sums available will be reduced. Some companies will also provide funds for clients with CCJs, losses and negative balance sheets, but the rates of interest will be considerably higher.

Commercial loans, including EFG loans

A perennial question is, should a company go for a commercial loan or overdraft? There is no simple answer; it depends on why you require the loan and for how long.

If the loan is for occasional short term use then an overdraft is normally cheaper to run and can be very flexible, but always keep at the back of your mind that an overdraft can be taken away overnight and this can have devastating effects.

If, however, you require the loan for long term use then a commercial loan is the safer option as it would be for a fixed term and fixed rate and unless you default it is much more difficult for the bank to cancel it. In today's market place be prepared for both an overdraft and a commercial loan to come with a requirement for Directors' personal guarantees.

The last Labour government introduced the Enterprise Finance Guarantee Scheme (EFGS). This type of loan was meant to be for those companies that were unable to back a loan with assets. In theory this is a great idea and should be invaluable for SMEs, but in practice, because the government also gave the banks discretion on whether or not to ask for personal guarantees, naturally in most cases the banks, being risk averse, are demanding PGs from directors. This is not always the case so do shop around, you may be lucky. In theory the EFG is supported by a 75% guarantee from the government to the banks, for which a 2% per annum surcharge is made on top of the bank's normal charges. To my mind if you are going to have to give PGs anyway, why pay 2% more for an EFG rather than try for a standard commercial loan?

If the EFG type loan is the only available loan for you then think out of the box. At the last count there were 40 providers of EFGs of which only 18 are banks. It pays to look around and especially take a look at the Invoice Discounters and Factors that also offer EFGs to their existing clients. They are often much more flexible than the high street banks.

If you are turned down for a loan do not give up. A client of mine was turned down for a small firm's loan guarantee loan, now called an EFG loan; he had asked for £100,000. He asked me to approach other lenders for him, which I was happy to do, but I first advised him to go back to his own bank and ask them to resubmit his request, but this time for £90,000. The loan was granted within two weeks.

Angel funding, both equity and debt

An important source of finance for growth companies is Business Angels. Business Angels come in many shapes and sizes and can be made up initially of the three Fs, family, friends and fools, as well as business contacts that you have made in the past and whose companies may have synergies with your own. As the business grows then 'professional' business angels come into play. Angels, by the nature of their activity, like to keep a low profile; there are naturally some exceptions such as those on Dragon's Den, and so the best way to make contact with them is through one of the many Angel Networks. Please do not think that Dragon's Den is typical of this type of funding. Most Angels are not dragons and are eager to help and offer constructive ideas and are on your side from the start.

Angel Networks may be either national or regional and may specialise in specific market areas or be very general in nature. Some work on a success fee only basis, usually around 5% of funds raised, while others charge an upfront fee as well as a success fee. It is not advisable to give your business plan to all and sundry as this can give the impression that you are desperate. It is important, however, not to put your eggs in one basket and my advice is to decide on one national network and one local network to start with. Remember that Angels not only provide capital for an equity stake in your company, they often will supply debt funding as well. Angels expect a high return on their investment, due to the risk that they are undertaking, so your business must be scalable to give them this return. There must also be a plausible exit strategy in place as they will want to see when and how they will get their capital and profit out again. The most likely and acceptable exit strategy is a trade sale, to a specific type of company, within 3–5 years. Angels will also be looking for an IRR of 35%+.

There is a new type of Angel Network, that has been popular in the USA but which is relatively new in the UK. These are the 'Crowdfunding Networks'. They are usually made up of ordinary people, small investors who may not normally invest in shares in unlisted companies. The amounts they invest can be as small as £100 or less. This type of network is proving very popular for start-up organisations that need funding. Crowdfunding also comes in two flavours, equity and debt, but the debt funding networks are only for companies that are three years old. Please see the section below for more information on Crowdfunding.

It is very important to be well prepared before you attempt to raise equity funding. Your business plan must be first class, to enable it to stand out from all the others that an Angel will read every week. Your management team must be ready and able to answer any questions that may be asked of them. Your forecast assumptions must be detailed, believable and understandable and your exit strategy must be clear. Too many business plans are just product and market place descriptions without detailed descriptions of how the company is actually going to operate. Most management teams have never been through this process before and so it is advisable to seek the help of a specialist who understands the process, who knows what Angels are looking for and how a business plan actually gets read and can prepare the company for most eventualities, as well as knowing many of the characters involved.

An often forgotten method of raising much needed capital in this difficult market place is to recruit a Non-Executive Chairman who is willing to invest into the organisation.

This type of recruitment is often done on a success fee only basis. A fee is charged for the actual recruitment and a second fee is charged for the investment made. You should also try to find someone who has an existing network of contacts within the client's market sector. You normally do not have to pay until the money is invested and then the charges come out of the investment.

Turnaround finance

Turnaround funding may not at first sight be seen as growth funding but in reality it is a very important source of funds for companies in desperate need of growth.

The most important sources of finance for good companies that for one reason or another have become distressed are the Turnaround Angel Networks that specialise in this type of funding. Companies that are in distress are normally in need of not only additional capital but also new ideas and new contacts. By approaching a specialist network of turnaround Business Angels, who can react very quickly, not only can new capital be provided but also new blood can be injected into the boardroom, with new ideas and also new business contacts and experience. This type of Angel is not normally interested in taking control of the company and can be a very valuable addition to the board. This is often a win/win situation. A common mistake that distressed companies make is to believe that they can undertake a pre-pack and emerge from the process without injecting new capital and new ideas, but if they do this then their chances of success are greatly reduced.

Invoice Discounting and Factoring is another useful source of funding in these circumstances as the company's past history is not as important as the credit worthiness of their debtors.

Many companies have 'forgotten assets'. These are assets that the MD may see every day but as they are totally owned by the company and often have been completely written off the balance sheet they are thought of as having no value. These assets may, however, still have a worthwhile capital value. If it has a useful working life left in it and a marketable second-hand value, then consider 'selling' it to a leasing company and then lease it back from them. You keep the use of the asset and also benefit from a capital injection. Once again it is the resale value of the asset on the second-hand market that is important to the leasing company, rather than the financial history of the company.

I had a client who phoned me up on Boxing Day one year. He was unable to enjoy his Christmas holiday because he knew that he could not pay the January wages due to poor sales in the autumn. He was, however, confident that his busy spring period would turn the company around. On investigation it was discovered that the company had 'forgotten' plant and machinery on its books that had already come off lease finance but still had significant second-hand value. The sale and lease back of these assets provided enough funds to pay the wage bill until sales improved. Without this funding the company would have had to close.

Crowdfunding

Crowdfunding is an alternative method of raising finance for a business project. Unlike traditional Angel investment, in which just a few people typically take a larger share in a business, with Crowdfunding an entrepreneur can attract a 'crowd' of people, who may not have invested in shares before, each of whom takes a small stake in a business idea, by contributing towards an online funding target.

Crowdfunding is not new. In 1997 fans underwrote an entire US tour for the British rock group Marillion by pooling their money. The film industry first used Crowdfunding in 2002 and a Trade Association for freelance workers raised £100,000 in 1999.

In the UK there are two main types of crowdfunding:

Equity crowdfunding is mainly used for funding start-ups where each investor receives an equity stake in the company, and **Debt crowdfunding,** which is not used for start-ups; the company has to be at least two years old and the money is a loan over 1, 3 or 5 years.

The main benefit of crowdfunding, other than raising much needed capital, is that it creates a strong network of support for your company. The equity model is especially good at creating ambassadors for your brand, promoting it amongst their networks, family and friends and often becoming returning customers themselves.

How does it work? Although the rules differ from site to site, generally an entrepreneur will pitch his/her idea, set a fundraising goal and set a deadline for raising funds. Potential lenders or investors can review the pitches and decide if there are any they would like to support. Many entrepreneurs will also offer incentives to investors in the form of discounts and special offers. If the total required is not raised then the funding does not go ahead. The procedure for a lending crowdfunding site is not quite the same. On these sites you have to decide what interest rate you want to receive and then you bid for a portion of the loan. A common mistake is for the loan applicants, when they see that they have achieved 100% funding, to take the money before the auction has actually finished. This results in them paying a higher interest rate than they need to. It must be remembered that this is an auction and when 100% of the funds have been raised, other potential lenders have to bid a lower interest rate to participate. I have seen loan rates decrease by over 2% in the last hours of an auction. So for the best results wait until the end of the auction before you take the funds raised.

How do I choose which crowdfunding site to use? Here are my **six top tips**:

- Choose the right site. Do you want equity or debt?
- Know your target audience and pitch accordingly.
- Plan ahead. A first class business plan is essential, good special offers for the investors are important and make certain you keep the interest going and have news items ready for each week of the investment cycle.
- Be passionate, include images and think seriously about a video to really get your message across.
- Make certain you explain exactly how the money is going to be spent.

- Do not leave it to the crowdfunding site to find all your investors for you. Leverage all your family and friends and publicise it on all your social networks. No one wants to be first to invest so make certain that a family member invests a small amount right at the beginning and keep the momentum going. It is easy to get investors at the end but difficult to get them at the beginning.

If you are a small start-up with a product that can catch the general public's imagination then equity crowdfunding may be the simplest and only way you may get your company up and running. If you are an established company but the bank will not lend to you, then debt crowdfunding could be the answer.

Crowdfunding is still only a small part of the fundraising scene in the UK, but it is growing fast and if the banks are not careful they will soon start to see a dent in their customer base. If you need funding then it is certainly worth your while looking into crowdfunding.

Conclusion

There are many funding providers in the marketplace today, the banks are not the only sources of funds and may not even be the best source for your needs. Look around the market, get specialist advice and makes certain you put the providers in competition with each other. There are sources of funding for most types of companies at whatever state of growth they are in, from concept, through growth and even in collapse.

Remember: 'Happiness is a positive Cash Flow'. Fred Adler.

Alan says:

I think Peter would agree with me when I emphasise the need to stay on side with your bank. Always consult them first on your finance needs and let them quote at every opportunity. If you can demonstrate you can achieve a better deal elsewhere, you can only gain their respect.

Remember the old adage: if people, by whom I mean customers, suppliers, investors and others, think you don't need them, they will want to help you all the more.

HOW THE LAW HELPS YOUR BUSINESS

Business Law and commercial thoughts

Toby Stroh

> My approach is that if the client wants
> my thoughts (as distinct from legal
> advice) on a given set of business
> circumstances then to the extent that I
> can help I am delighted to do so.

How the Law Helps your Business

This chapter is not intended to be a learned treatise on matters legal that relate to entrepreneurs. Entire books are written on such matters. Rather, it is intended to demonstrate that there are many common challenges and just as many ways of approaching them. None is necessarily wrong. Or right.

But by way of some tips and traps:

Early Legal Advice is Good Legal Advice: get a lawyer on board soon

Sometimes, just sometimes, it happens that people seek legal advice before taking steps that might make life difficult. Not often enough but it does happen.

Romeo and Juliet got in touch with me (whilst I was writing this chapter as it happens) and said they had been recommended to me by another client of mine who told them that they needed some sound commercial advice. They are two high-powered people in the financial services world who wanted to set up their own business. The precise nature of the business doesn't matter for the purposes of this story. What does matter is that they came to me before any key decisions were taken.

The fact that this was a new, start-up business is relevant in at least one way but some of the issues that arise are relevant at any stage in the life-cycle of an existing, developing business that is seeking to go to the "next stage".

So back to Romeo and Juliet who are currently on garden leave. (I mention garden leave further below but please note at this stage that what is key to bear in mind is that if you are on garden leave you are still employed by your employer. Try to consider it as simply working out your notice period sitting in your garden rather than at work).

Just how free am I to do what I want to do?

I told them that there are at least two aspects to consider at this stage: first, how to avoid the traps and pitfalls of leaving employment and entering a potentially competing arena; and second, what to bear in mind when setting up their new business.

With regard to the first aspect I asked them whether they had downloaded any information from their current employer and told them in no uncertain terms that if they had done so this was potentially very awkward. I also told them that they should not do so at any stage in the future.

I told them that they should not, as many people do, consider the post-termination restraints (in their contracts of employment) as not worth the paper on which they are written. This is frequently not the case and can be a very costly mistake.

Post-termination restraints are those provisions in your

employment contract that, for example, seek to restrict your ability to set up business in competition or try to do business with their employer's customers.

Avoid any fights

If you are starting up a new business you can rarely afford either the time or the money that is necessary to go to court and have a fight with anyone.

Also, I told them that they must be very careful not to use their employer's confidential information. Although it is sometimes difficult to define what is, in fact, confidential information there are certain categories or types of information that, generally speaking, are obviously confidential (pricing, new product lines, financials are some examples).

So, having talked through these basic issues with Romeo and Juliet we then spoke about the rather more constructive reason for their coming to see me, namely how to set up their new business.

That brought me on to one of the most important aspects of helping a business, whether it is a start-up or one that is developing, and that is making sure that whatever structures and arrangements are put in place (or, in the case of an existing business, are later put into place to assist a new business to go to the next level) they have to be robust, sensible and workable.

But Romeo and Juliet, being relatively sophisticated individuals, had plugged into information with which they were already slightly familiar relating to structuring of a business and had already set about drafting (or, rather, amending) an existing document they had obtained from other sources.

But how do I get there?

I told them that this was fine but that sometimes it was more efficient on all fronts (cost and time) to start from scratch. I used my example of being stopped at a particular tube station and being asked how to get to another station. Well, I sometimes say, if I were you I wouldn't start from here. In this particular case, as it happens, the draft was certainly usable.

And what structure should I use?

This, then, brought us on to structure and which type of vehicle was the best for their particular purposes. Due, partly, to the type of business they are in they had opted for a limited liability partnership ("LLP"), a relatively new creation with certain pluses and certain minuses. Although LLPs were originally introduced to benefit professional partnerships (accountants) they are now used in many different businesses for different reasons.

Most business people will try to maximise their protection from personal liability if things go wrong with their business (whether through the supply of bad services or products or through bad financial management).

Get a good accountant on board as soon as possible

One of the other key issues for businesses (again, whether start up or developing) is to have the right type and level of financial and taxation advice. Romeo and Juliet didn't have any particular contacts with accountants operating or specialising in their field of activity so I was able to give them a couple of names of firms that I knew would be able to help them.

Getting back to the nature of the vehicle Romeo and Juliet had chosen, the LLP, I said that whilst this basic structure was very much the norm in their field of activity there were, even then, many variations on how LLPs can be set up so as to maximise potential tax benefits.

Taxation matters

Taxation is one of the most important considerations in any business, whether new or developing, and is an area that needs to be kept constantly under review. This is where a proactive (but not aggressively so) firm of accountants can add considerable value and is most valuable.

I then discussed with Romeo and Juliet how they planned to staff their business. They said that they anticipated having some additional members (partners) of the LLP but also some employees.

Employees matter, too

So, this then led on to a question and answer session about what they should be looking for and how best to achieve it.

The touchstone of reasonableness in employee relations

I told them that whatever was written into any employment

contract, what is fundamental to the relationship between employee and employer is that the employer must act reasonably. Using that as a touchstone and really adhering to it would mean that most of the problems that employers typically meet would be avoided.

And the importance of relevancy in employment contracts

That said, they need to have clear written contracts which are relevant for the particular type of employee. There is no point having a full-blown service agreement for administrative staff any more that it would be sensible to have a skeleton template for a senior employee. All contracts of employment have to be relevant and clear.

The higher the level of employee the greater the level of protection Romeo and Juliet will need to protect the legitimate business interests of their LLP. So, certainly, they – like their own current employers did with their own contracts – should put into the contracts bespoke provisions relating to confidential information, post-termination restraints and other provisions relevant to the particular industry in which they operate.

I pointed out that the employer protection pendulum has relatively recently swung back in favour of them, as the qualifying period before employees gain the right not to be unfairly dismissed went up from one to two years for new employees. I haven't yet gone into the legal backdrop of the distinction between unfair and wrongful dismissal, due to the concern of information overload.

I asked them whether they had thought about how long they

intended to run the business and how they might realise the value of the business they were setting up.

Just how important am I or should I be to the business?

I told them that in a way this is like writing a will when relatively young. You anticipate and, in a way, recognise your own mortality. What they need to do is to create a business that will run without them – they need to be able to write themselves out of the business – as that is the only way they will create a capital asset for them to sell in the future. Not an easy thing to do at an early stage, but vital.

Finally, Romeo and Juliet asked whether we could meet up in the not too distant future to talk about premises and other commercial contracts that they would need to have in place.

So, that then is a fairly typical first round meeting covering some of the key issues in any start-up business.

The legal and regulatory environment relating to start-up and growing businesses is complex and a business owner should always maintain a bird's eye view of the legal framework applicable to his business, and should also consider seeking professional advice on matters which may be unfamiliar or of concern.

For those of you who would like to know a little more about some of the types of structures that are commonly used and the legal backdrop to them, I have set out as an appendix to this chapter some information that you might find helpful.

More key issues

Well, said Romeo and Juliet, when they came back to see me a short while later. That is all very well but what happens next?

Next stages and what to anticipate?

I told them that it is unlikely that they would be able to run their business on their own. Or if they were to do so, it will reach its critical mass all too soon.

With this in mind I suggested to Romeo and Juliet that they consider the possibility of binding some or all of their employees into the business. The "incentivise, motivate and retain" mantra was discussed, as were the benefits of commonality of interest. They took this on board and said they would find out more about the nature and types of co-ownership or other shared arrangements.

We discussed the various cycles within any business venture. There are no "check-lists" that can prepare the entrepreneur on an on-going basis. Rather, they will plateau and realise when they get there that they somehow need to move forward to the next level and then the next plateau.

The trick is to anticipate the plateau that will inevitably arrive and work out how to overcome the hurdles before you fall over them.

I said that it was most likely that the next time we had a discussion about structure was likely to be when the business was a success and other people were interested in "helping" them take it forward.

Don't give too much away: the perils of accepting external investment.

I told them about a highly successful businessman who had, in the early days of his business, been approached by a number of banks who saw the potential upside of his business, the potential synergies between their businesses and, most importantly from the bank's perspective, the relative inequality of bargaining power between my client, the markets they could open to him and the enormous potential benefits for him.

To cut a relatively long story short the banks – or at least one in particular – overplayed its hand and my client went forward on his own. The bank required a far higher share of the equity than my client was prepared to give up. This was easy for me and my client's number two to see but not particularly for my client, himself, to see. He worked extremely hard and became extremely wealthy and made a large number of his employees very wealthy as well.

But certainly as a lesson for Romeo and Juliet to take on board, the ability of their advisors to challenge and support as appropriate when others are seeking to enter into joint arrangements, is key.

And don't forget to protect what you create.

Speak to your legal advisor, trade mark or patent agent before you do anything else. Confidentiality is key.

If you remember that concept then you should not go wrong. Then before divulging information to other third parties make sure that you do so under a non-disclosure agreement (frequently referred to as an "NDA").

Indeed, it is not uncommon for the more sophisticated investor to refuse to review information that might be commercially sensitive or capable of commercial exploitation without having entered into an NDA.

Whilst this might seem odd, the fact is that some recipients of such information have had their fingers burned by individuals who claim rights to products of such recipients arguing that they, the individuals, were directly or indirectly responsible for the success of the recipient. One of the better ways of recipients protecting themselves against such accusations is to be able to demonstrate that their invariable practice is to receive such information under an NDA, leaving it up to the individual to produce it if it exists.

Not ideal, but such an approach actually benefits both individual and potential exploiter or business partner.

Trusted business advisors, horses and water

I told Romeo and Juliet that some legal advisors have the experience, skill-sets, desire and willingness to contribute more to the client's business than simply setting what I call the "legal backdrop".

That is not, however, to deny the importance of the legal backdrop as it is the content of that backdrop – together with all other relevant matters – that a client will review when reaching a decision.

I pointed out before they did that not all clients welcome non-legal input. Quite a few will simply want the lawyer to give the clearest possible and definitive legal advice (and that is certainly not anywhere as easy as it should be – but that is a whole other story) to feed into what is the melting pot of the client's mind.

That is one extreme.

Slightly to the left of that position is the client who wants pure legal input but accepts – say on a scale of 1 to 10 – how likely it is that the downside (or upside) might materialise.

Then the farthest to the left on the scale is the client who wants to share with the legal advisor his thought processes so that you can analyse and dissect – or stress-test if you will – the set of circumstances facing the client at the particular time.

I told Romeo and Juliet that becoming a client's trusted business advisor, someone who the client will go to before taking key decisions – is not something that all legal advisors are prepared to do. Some take the view that this is outside their comfort zone or skill sets, experience or expertise. All perfectly valid arguments.

My approach, however, having been round the block a few times and been involved sometimes extremely closely in the running of clients' businesses, is that if the client wants to ask for my thoughts or comments on a given set of circumstances relating to his business, then to the extent that I can help I am delighted to do so.

I told Romeo and Juliet that clients – like legal advisors – come in all shapes and sizes (metaphorically and physically) and that some will look askance or be put out by the thought of my straying outside what those particular clients consider to be my remit of straight legal advice.

Others, however, will pick up the phone to keep me up to date on developments so that they can then discuss with me, if and when the situation arises, what is best for his business.

I ended up this particular part of my discussion with Romeo and Juliet by referring to the fluid and dynamic nature of the solicitor/client relationship and that the nature and level of input from me as their legal advisor must be their choice and theirs alone.

To the extent that there is no check-list for running a business the closest that most entrepreneurs will get to getting advice and assistance on an on-going basis is through their trusted business advisors, whether they be legal advisors or accountants. Both should be equally important in the life-cycle of any business.

How far can we future-proof our business?

Another interesting question from Romeo and Juliet anticipating, as it did, the central theme in this book as previously alluded to.

I told them that my view is that you cannot do so completely. What you can, however, do to afford yourself maximum protections, I told them (and this is, in fact, the central tenet of this discussion), is to put in place (***before*** the business gets up and running as afterwards is always too late) the all-important foundations of a sound business (nature and structure) and to have around you trusted business advisors who are willing and able to act as sounding-boards for you and who understand your particular business and business in general.

I told them also, to beware the active investor. This is, in fact, a variation on the "don't give away too much" theme referred to above, albeit in a very different context.

I explained to Romeo and Juliet how one of my other clients, Julius, operates. He was a highly successful individual in the financial services industry who together with a couple of pals set up a fund to invest in tech-based university spin-outs. All very bright, extremely hard-working individuals who wanted to create a portfolio of a relatively small number of companies, add value to them through their active participation and then realise their investments through some form of exit (see further below in this chapter and elsewhere in this book).

To cut short another fairly long and not particularly edifying story, the model was not the success the participants had hoped for or anticipated.

There was absolutely no lack of commitment on the part of the investors – indeed their individual contributions, particularly from a time and commitment basis were astonishing – but the model did not work.

My view is that it didn't work – and is not likely to work – due to the blurring of too many boundaries.

If you want to have a highly-experienced Chairman or CEO or CFO or COO or Sales Director and you want to give him equity in the business then that is fine, as is giving him some fairly standard minority protections relating to his minority equity holding.

What you should not, however, do, I cautioned the by now rather beleaguered Romeo and Juliet, is to let that person, through shareholder or other equity control be able to determine the fundamentals of the business.

This is quite an extraordinarily complex balancing act, but what is clear is that Romeo and Juliet – and all the other entrepreneurs who are out there with their ideas, plans and expectations – must have effective proprietorship of their creation. Of course there will be elements of control that can be imposed and accepted, but lose that feeling of proprietorship and you may as well pack up your tents at a very early stage.

The other end of this fulcrum, however, and hence the extraordinarily complex balancing act, is the need for the Romeos and Juliets of this entrepreneurial world which they have chosen to inhabit to accept that the closer to the business are the external investors, the greater the element of control they are likely to require for their investment.

The way to minimise the tensions and balancing issues that I raised above with Romeo and Juliet is to delineate as tightly as possible the roles of the investing protagonists. And that, I told them, is a real art.

Is the lady about to stop singing and other exit analogies?

Returning now to one of the points that I made to Romeo and Juliet, one of the main points about creating your own business is considering your exit strategy. The earlier you think about this the better.

With this in mind I set out below some pointers for consideration.

There are various methods by which an entrepreneur may exit from the company with the preferred one very much depending on the nature of the business and the needs and wishes of the entrepreneur. Each route has its advantages and disadvantages and may be subject to different tax treatment.

The entrepreneur should obtain full professional advice before selecting the form of exit which will be most suitable for them, but by way of an overview, the routes available include: a trade sale, flotation, share sale and asset (or business) sale.

Commenting briefly on each (whole books are written on each topic so this is merely a very simple summary):

Trade

In a trade sale, the entire share capital of the Company is sold by its shareholders to a trade purchaser, which is a third party who is involved in the same business as the Company. This has a number of advantages; most significantly it usually allows the entrepreneur to exit the company in full and immediately. This form of exit is often relatively quick and straightforward. The main disadvantage is that it frequently involves negotiating with a competitor, as part of which the disclosure of confidential and sensitive material will be required.

Flotation

Flotation occurs where shares of a company commence trading on a public stock market. Generally, this will be accompanied by a primary offering by the Company of its shares to new investors.

However, the entrepreneur only makes a return on the sale of his shares. Often a substantial part of the entrepreneur's holding is sold some time after the initial flotation as incoming investors expect to see existing investors maintaining their position, and consequently interest, in the company.

Although this exit route is likely to maximise the value of the entrepreneur's holding, and enable him to remain in operational control, it is the longest and most costly exit route. Its success is also dependent on market conditions and it is not suitable for every business.

Share

This option is similar to a trade sale, albeit that the purchaser is not involved in the same business as the company. In a share sale, the company's shares are transferred from the entrepreneur to the purchaser. This means that the business is purchased as a going concern and its assets are acquired together with any liabilities and obligations. A share sale, therefore, enables the entrepreneur to dispose of his business in full, although the deal may be structured so that he retains some involvement in the management or ownership for a specified period.

An entrepreneur who exits through a share sale will retain a degree of ongoing liability. This, however, is limited to the warranties and indemnities it gives to the buyer, the extent of which it can negotiate.

Asset

Instead of selling shares in the company, the entrepreneur may sell the company's assets. However, unlike with a share sale, in this form of exit only the assets and liabilities which the buyer agrees to obtain are purchased. This has its advantages where the business's value is tied up in its assets or where the entrepreneur only wishes to sell part of the business.

The possibility of an asset sale not achieving the entire disposal of the business is one disadvantage. Another disadvantage of an asset sale is that they are often more complex than a share sale due to the need to transfer each of the separate assets constituting the business. It usually also involves obtaining more consents and approvals, for example, in relation to the assignment or novation of existing contracts.

Other Options

In addition to the above forms of exit, the entrepreneur may decide to pass the business on to his family or sell the company to managers or employees. The latter is known as a management buyout. Alternatively the entrepreneur could simply decide to close the business and wind it up, an option which is not just available to an insolvent company.

APPENDIX – the techno bit

For those of you who like boxes and lists I set out below some that are intended to make you feel you have read something substantive.

As I said at the beginning of this chapter, this was not intended as a learned treatise on legal issues. Rather, it was intended as setting out some thoughts that are likely to pass across the minds of entrepreneurs from time to time.

Limited or Unlimited Liability

Sole Trader and Partnership – overview	
Advantages	Disadvantages
Flexible; No formality in setting up; Low administrative running requirements; No publicly available accounts or other details.	Lack of limited liability; No separate legal personality so unable to hold property or enter into contracts in its own name.

Limited Liability

Shares – the benefits
The benefits of shares include: New shares may be issued to obtain investment in the company; Different classes of shares may be issued. For example shares which have a right to a dividend without carrying voting rights. This way new investment is obtained without diluting the existing shareholders' control.

Limited Company - overview

Limited Company - overview	
Advantages	Disadvantages
Limited liability for shareholders; Separate legal personality so the company can enter into contracts and own assets in its name; Prestige of and trust in a limited company.	Administrative requirements – some documents need to be filed annually, such as accounts and a return, others are on the occurrence of a particular event; "double taxation" on profits drawn as dividends. The company pays corporation tax.

Limited Liability Partnerships (LLPs)

Limited Liability Partnerships - overview	
Advantages	Disadvantages
Limited liability for members; Separate legal personality so the LLP can enter into contracts and own assets in its name; Protection of name – an LLP's name is allocated on incorporation; Flexibility – there are fewer statutory requirements than with a company giving members more scope to decide what they want; Tax transparency.	Administrative requirements – some documents need to be filed annually, such as accounts and a return, others are on the occurrence of a particular event; The requirement to file annual accounts which are available for public inspection; Relatively new and, therefore, relatively unknown quantity.

Shareholders' Agreements

Shareholders' Agreement – content
The content of shareholders' agreements varies depending on the parties and the size and nature of the company, for example. Some of the usual provisions are: The company's business (which may include the requirement to produce an annual business plan);   Who the company's directors are to be, their management responsibilities and how meetings are to be conducted;   How the company is to be financed;   Dividend policies;   Restrictions on the shareholders (such as to not compete with the company's business whilst he is a shareholder and for a finite period afterwards);   Deadlock on decisions; and   Requirements on the transfer of shares (such as to offer them to the other shareholders before being able to sell to a third party).

LLP Agreements

Unlike with companies, LLPs are not required to have a constitution and there are relatively few statutory rules governing their management. Like with partnerships, how its business is run and managed are matters for the members to decide for themselves and to include in an agreement. Whilst there is no requirement to have an LLP agreement the lack of one is usually extremely problematic if the members should, for example, fall out, or if a member dies or wants to leave. As there is no agreement in place to govern what should happen in such circumstances, expensive and drawn-out disputes can occur. Again it is important to put such agreements in place early on.

Also, in the absence of a written LLP Agreement certain

"default provisions" will be implied often with unexpected and unwelcome consequences. For example, if there is no written LLP Agreement the profits (and losses) of the LLP will be shared (and borne) equally. Something that may not have been intended by the members.

LLP Agreement – content

LLP Agreement – content
LLP Agreements will generally prescribe such issues as: the proportions in which the members own the business; The members' capital contributions; Banking and accounting matters; Who is entitled to the profits; Who is liable for the losses; Insurance; The LLP's property; Retirement and death; Expulsion from the LLP; and The management functions and responsibilities of the members.

Agency and distribution

Appointing an agent – the benefits
Appointing an agent to act on behalf of a business has numerous advantages, in particular: An agent will usually know the particular sales market and already have a client following; The agent will only receive a commission if he actually obtains orders; Since the agent is usually only acting as an intermediary, the principal will also come to know the clients; and The principal can leave the agent to sell and secure orders, freeing up the principal's time.

Under a distribution agreement, the supplier or manufacturer sells his products to a distributor, who then sells the products on to his customers in his own name and on his own behalf, adding a margin to cover his own costs and give him his profit. Contrast this with the agency position where the only contract for sale of the products is made between the principal and the end customer. The agent generally has no contractual liability to the customer.

Appointing a distributor – key points
The distribution route has a number of benefits: The distributor bears the risk of any unsold goods; The distributor will usually know the sales market; The business will only have to deal with one customer, the distributor, and there will be a lower risk of bad debts; The distributor will bear the burden of any problems; and The business will save a lot of additional work, such as administration and after sales guarantees and service.

Two potential and popular methods of expanding business into new markets or territories are agency and distribution agreements. Although these two methods may initially appear similar, it is important for a business, when considering how best to market, sell or distribute its products, to be aware of the difference, in legal and practical terms, between appointing an agent and a distributor.

Under an agency agreement, an agent is appointed by the principal to negotiate and possibly conclude contracts with customers on the principal's behalf. He is paid commission on the sales he makes, usually on a percentage basis.

EMPLOYMENT MATTERS

Employment Particulars

Employees in the UK enjoy a wide range of employment rights one of which is that, an employee who has been working for an employer for more than one month has the right to receive a written statement of employment particulars. This must be provided by the employer within two months of the employee starting work and must set out the main employment rights.

Written statement of employment particulars – prescribed terms

The terms prescribed by statute to be included in a written statement of employment particulars are:

The names of the employer and employee;
The date when the employment began;
The date on which the employee's period of continuous employment began;
The scale or rate of remuneration or the method of calculating remuneration;
The intervals at which remuneration is paid;
Any terms and conditions relating to hours of work;
Terms and conditions relating to: entitlement to holidays; incapacity for work due to sickness or injury; pensions and pension schemes; the length of notice which the employee is obliged to give and entitled to receive to terminate his contract of employment; the title of the job which the employee is employed to do; where the employment is not intended to be permanent, the period for which it is expected to continue or, if it is for a fixed term, the date when it is to end; the place of work; and
Any collective agreements which directly affect the terms and conditions of the employment.

Contracts of Employment

An employment contract is an agreement between an employer and an employee which sets out the employee's employment rights, responsibilities and duties. There is no set form and the contract may either be oral or written. Although there is no legal requirement to provide an employee with a contract of employment (not to be confused with a written statement of particulars), setting out the terms of the relationship in writing creates certainty.

In addition to the terms expressed in the contract of employment, there is a number of terms implied in the contract. For the employer, many of these are discussed in the heading of "employer responsibilities" below.

Implied Terms - Employee

Terms implied into the employee's contract include:
 	
    The duty of good faith and fidelity;
    The duty not to compete with the employer;
    The duty of confidentiality;
    The duty to obey reasonable and lawful orders;
    The duty to be adaptable;
    The duty to exercise reasonable care and skill; and
    Professional obligations (which will vary according to the employee's role).

Employer responsibilities

In addition to the duties expressed in the employee's contract of employment, employers have a number of additional responsibilities in relation to their employees. Although some of these may appear to be obvious, they are important and must be observed by all employers.

Employer's responsibilities

Employer's responsibilities
The obligation to pay wages – this includes the duty not to make any unlawful deductions from an employee's wages; The duty to provide work. There is no general obligation on an employer to provide work for the employee so long as their wages are paid. However, a right to work may be implied into the contract where the employee is otherwise deprived of the opportunity of earning remuneration. For example, where remuneration includes a piece-work rate, shift premium or commission; Health and safety – an employer has a duty to take reasonable care of the health and safety of employees, which includes mental as well as physical health; The duty to provide a suitable working environment; The duty to promptly redress any employee grievances; and The implied term of mutual trust and confidence.

The rights of employees and duties on employers are extensive and many may be new to the owners of start-up businesses. Because of the many pitfalls for the unaware, businesses are strongly advised to seek legal advice on all employment matters at the earliest possible stage

Dismissal

One of the fundamental rights an employee enjoys is the right not to be unfairly dismissed. To qualify for this, employees need to have at least one year's continuous service if they were in employment before 6 April 2012 or two years' continuous service if their employment commenced on or after 6 April 2012. There is, however, an exception – where the employee was dismissed for an automatically unfair reason no period of continuous service is required.

Unfair Dismissal – Some automatically unfair reasons

Unfair Dismissal – Some automatically unfair reasons
Dismissals are classed as 'automatically unfair' if the reason or principal reason for the dismissal is that the employee exercises specific employment rights including: For reasons connected with pregnancy, childbirth, statutory maternity, paternity parental and adoption leave or dependant care leave; in connection with time off for study and training request rights or carrying out jury service; For performing functions as an employee representative; For a health and safety reason; Related to the national minimum wage or in connection with an application for flexible working; Related to status as a part-time worker or fixed-term employee; In connection with trade union recognition, for participation in trade union activities or trade union membership or non-membership; and in connection with exercising prescribed rights as an agency worker.

As a result of the protection afforded to employees, an entrepreneur seeking to dismiss an employee should take care to ensure that dismissal is undertaken in a way which does not constitute unfair dismissal. This requires the employer to have a fair reason for the dismissal and act reasonably in treating that as the reason for dismissal.

Fair Reasons

There are five potentially fair reasons for dismissal:

Redundancy

This occurs where there is a business closure (employer ceases or intends to cease to carry on the business for the purposes of which the employee was employed by him); a workplace closure (where the business is the place where the employee was employed ceases), or there is a reduced need for the number of employees (the requirements of that business for employees to either carry out work of a particular kind or to carry out work of a particular kind in the place where the employee was employed by the employer have ceased or diminished or are expected to cease or diminish).

The Employee's Capability or Qualifications

Legislation states that capability in the context of unfair dismissal requires an assessment by reference to an employee's "skill, aptitude, health or any other physical or mental quality". In practice, dismissals under this category will either be by reason of an employee's ill health, or because of their poor performance or attitude.

A fair dismissal for qualifications could arise where it emerges that, after being recruited, the employee does not in fact have the necessary qualifications or the employee fails to obtain the qualifications which they were employed on the understanding of obtaining.

The Employee's Conduct

Misconduct by the employee, either through multiple acts or, if sufficiently serious, a single act (gross misconduct) may be a fair reason for dismissal. Examples of misconduct include theft or fraud, violence at work, misuse of computers or unauthorised absence. Where misconduct is alleged, it is important that the employer carries out as much investigation of the offence as is reasonable in the circumstances.

Statutory Restriction

Sometimes this potentially fair reason for dismissal is referred to as illegality. It arises where the employee cannot continue to work in the position which he held without contravention, either on the part of the employee or his employer, of a duty or restriction imposed by or under an enactment. This would, for example, catch dismissals where immigration rules would be breached by continued employment, the employee is required to drive to do his job and loses his driving licence or the employee gains a criminal record.

Some Other Substantial Reason ("SOSR")

This is often referred to as the "catch all" provision under which fair dismissals not otherwise falling under the above categories are caught. The most common form of an SOSR dismissal is where the employer undergoes a business restructuring by which work of a particular kind does not diminish, but it is allocated differently within the business, resulting in job losses.

Reasonableness of the Dismissal and Fair Procedure

Where the employer has a fair reason for dismissing the employee, the employer must also act reasonably in treating this as a reason for dismissal for it to be fair. This is assessed by asking whether in the circumstances (including the size and administrative resources of the employer's undertaking) the employer acted reasonably or unreasonably in treating it as a sufficient reason for dismissing the employee. In addition regard is had to equity and the substantial merits of the case.

The test as to whether or not the employer acted reasonably is an objective one. The assessment is whether the employer's decision to dismiss the employee fell within the range of reasonable responses that a reasonable employer in those circumstances and in that business might have adopted.

In order to act reasonably, an employer must follow a fair procedure when dismissing an employee. For dismissals relating to misconduct and poor performance, the Code of Practice produced by ACAS is explicitly said to apply. This requires the employer to investigate the issues, inform the employee of the issues in writing, conduct a disciplinary hearing or meeting with the employee and inform the employee of the decision in writing.

Discrimination

Legislation is in place to protect people from discrimination or harassment in respect of one or more of nine characteristics (protected characteristics). Broadly, an employer must not discriminate against a person in the arrangements he makes for deciding to whom to offer employment, as to the terms on which he offers the person employment and by not offering the person employment. Once employed, an employer must not discriminate against an employee as to employment terms, in the way they do or don't afford the employee access to opportunities for promotion, transfer or training or for receiving any other benefit, facility or service or by dismissing the employee.

Discrimination – the Protected Characteristics
Age Disability Gender reassignment Marriage and civil partnership Pregnancy and maternity. Race Religion or belief Sex Sexual orientation

Alan says:

It is pretty obvious that it's best to be prepared for circumstances demanding legal intervention rather than wait for the problem to arise and then consult a lawyer. A clear example would be when setting up a business partnership so that initial enthusiasm does not outweigh common sense in agreeing terms.

The same is also true for taking on substantial investment requiring dilution of equity. Consult your advisers before getting too excited about the opportunity.

The advantage already emphasised in this chapter of having a legal adviser who is able and willing to give some early thoughts on an issue, may just save you money and perhaps more importantly help you avoid a wrong decision.

MARKETING YOUR BUSINESS TO THE NEXT LEVEL

Victoria Ash and Paul Griffith

Marketing is useful shorthand for everything you need to do to generate revenue (and profit) in your business.

Marketing your business to the next level

You are an established entrepreneur so you are obviously doing something right when it comes to marketing and business development, or you would have already gone under!

The challenge we're looking at is how to grow your business to the next level. Where do you start, especially if you don't have a marketing background? With so many tactical activities on offer, how do you decide what's right for you and your business as it moves into the next phase of development? This chapter helps you change direction by focusing on just three issues that can be roughly summarised as Why, What and Who.

Why are you doing it – what's your firm's **marketing mind-set** and your long-term vision for your business? How you look at marketing makes the biggest difference to what results you get.

What are the **marketing decisions** that will **deliver return on investment?** We'd like to share a tool we use to simplify all the tactical choices you will have to make. Do you need to do PR? What about social media marketing? Or maybe you need to research your clients more?

Who is going to make it happen? How do you go about assembling a good **marketing team?**

This is not a chapter on how to do basic marketing activities. If you want to move your marketing to the next level we'll show you that it's about rising above the "how do I do it?" challenges and having the mind-set to answer the Why, What and Who.

Section 1

The Marketing Mindset

Every business gives a slightly different interpretation to the word 'marketing'. For some, it's a 'cost-centre' of little strategic importance: a function that spends money on brochures, coasters, pens and umbrellas, and often is first to suffer when savings need to be made. For others, it's more strategic but removed from the day-to-day business of generating new customers (the responsibility of 'sales'), or looking after existing clients (possibly the account team's baby). **For us, 'marketing' is useful shorthand for everything you do to generate revenue (and profit) in your business.** This means the whole spectrum of activity you might undertake to find new business, convert opportunities and deliver to clients. Equally importantly, 'marketing' is both a function in your business, with staff, budgets, processes and reporting lines, but it's also about the culture and 'attitude' you want to build.

*Why does marketing matter to your business? Chances are that, day-to-day, it's all about new business, particularly in these cash-strapped times. In small businesses marketing investment usually has to be carefully weighed in terms of the short-term revenue gain it's likely to generate. In this section we want you to start thinking about why someone would buy your **business** as well as about why people buy your products or services. Understanding what is really being bought will put a different shine on your marketing. There's marketing that just buys you a little more customer attention and then there's marketing that fundamentally makes your business more attractive to a buyer than any other business. Understand the difference and you are more likely to make the right marketing choices to drive your business to a new level.*

> "Buyers will pay more for a business that has good revenue generating capabilities."

Increase Your Business's Value

Valuing a business is a complex matter, and there are a number of different methods of doing so but, at heart, they all depend on the profitability and the assets of the company, often subject to an industry multiple. While you may not be able to change the industry multiple that applies in your sector, you can affect whether buyers see you as worth more or less than this standard multiple.

Among other things, buyers will pay more for a business that has:

- a clear position (people know what the business is famous for)
- valuable revenue-generating skills
- the ability to develop new markets and new products
- unique intellectual property (IP)

All of these are "marketing" capabilities. Each can be used to leverage the purchaser's existing business. If you don't have these attributes, it's a fair bet that you are only being bought for your turnover and the buyer will be looking to pay less than the industry multiple. See more on this subject in the chapter 'Choose your exit strategy'.

Generating clients and repeat business to improve long term profitability

As a result of the recession many businesses are now taking a much more sophisticated approach to their marketing. In the past, many SMEs relied on their direct sales force to knock on as many doors as possible but, in today's tough market, many are realising that they need to do something different, and our bet is that this need will continue well after the end of the recession.

That 'difference' can involve a huge range of options, from integrated thematic campaigns, to email marketing and telemarketing, or perhaps a better focus on your existing client base to generate more revenue at lower cost through repeat sales.

Where the long-term value comes is in recognising that great marketing involves both creativity and organisation. What do we mean by this? Creativity isn't necessarily about being 'whacky'. Sure, printing your law firm's name on condom wrappers and distributing them in night clubs (true story) might earn you recognition but are you really reaching the right people at the right time? For most of us true creativity is about getting inside your customers' shoes, and understanding what makes them tick. It's about appreciating their needs and wants, and providing a distinctive, cost-effective way to meet them.

Creativity on its own isn't enough though. What creates long-term profitability is the ability to build a marketing 'engine-room' that takes creative ideas and makes them work, time and time again. This means building a skilled team, systems, processes and measurement, so that you know that if you put the raw material of creativity in at one end, you will generate profitable sales on a regular basis at the other.

Staff and skills

As we've said above, 'marketing' isn't just a function; it's part of truly successful companies' culture. It's about being customer-oriented, flexible and creative, whether you work in sales, production or accounts. As you think about how to build the long-term value of your business, how closely are you considering how you build that culture and a marketing skillset among your employees? Growing the revenue of the business shouldn't just be seen as the responsibility of the marketing team.

What should be their responsibility, however, is thinking about how to transfer their skills into the rest of your business, so that everyone is aware of how they can contribute to the growth of the company. At this point you may be thinking, how does this apply to, say, my credit controller? If repeat business is important to your company, then every client interaction counts – including debt collection.

In conclusion, marketing is both a function and a 'state of mind' and plays a vital role in building the equity value of a successful business as well as helping it to achieve a new level of performance.

Section 2

What marketing should I be doing?

Good marketing strategy is all about focus and setting your priorities to help you make good marketing decisions.

How good is your marketing strategy? Do you have any comfort that you've got the right plans in place? Or are you like many businesses, whose sales and marketing strategy is often determined by:

- *What we've always done*
- *What's cheapest*
- *The wish list we came up with in a brainstorm*
- *What people feel like doing today*

Or, as one client recently described it, "The latest shiny thing to come along".

The reality is that there are so many different tactical things you could be doing, from advertising to networking; from cold calling to social media; from market research to PR. While none of them is 'wrong', how do you work out what's right for your business? It's one of the commonest requests for help that we get. It's this ability to make good marketing decisions quickly that makes the difference. And being able to prioritise all the good ideas that come your way is at the heart of making good decisions.

So, how do you work out where you should focus now, and in the longer term? We've developed a tool that we use to run workshops on this topic, often in conjunction with feedback from clients, suppliers and staff. We call it the Nine Box Matrix:

FIND	CONVERT	DELIVER
POSITION	BUYERS JOURNEY	PRODUCT / SERVICES
CAPABILITY	COMMUNI-CATION	CLIENT MANAGEMENT
CHANNEL	STARTING CONVERSATIONS	CLIENT SERVICE

We'll discuss this in more detail later, but broadly speaking the Nine Box Matrix represents the nine core areas of revenue generation grouped under three main headings: *finding business, converting leads into sales* and *delivering to clients*.

For a bit of fun – which will also give you an insight into where you need to prioritise – we've redesigned it in the guise of a light quiz. It will tell you whether your marketing strategy is Dynamite, Dabbling or a Damp Squib. And will make it clear where you should focus for the next stage of revenue growth. Do this as a serious exercise and you'll find making marketing decisions much easier. You'll know if the 'latest shiny thing' really meets your needs or not.

> "Do you know where you are on the business life-cycle? It will determine whether your focus should be on Finding, Converting or Delivering to Clients.

One extra thought: your focus will depend on a variety of factors – not simply the areas where you score less well, but where you are in your business life-cycle. A start-up business, for example, will want to put more emphasis on *Finding sources of revenue*, while a mature business will be concentrating on *Delivering to existing clients* and ensuring repeat business.

As you work through the quiz, score each question using the scheme below:

✓   = working well; no need to change

–   = not great but not terrible either

✗   = not working well; needs fixing

We suggest you score your business initially in a fairly instinctive (i.e., fast) fashion, reviewing your choices in a more considered manner later if necessary.

Positioning – what makes you different to your competitors?

		✓, – or ✗
1	Have you reviewed and defined what you are known for in the last 2 years?	
2	Do you feel your business has an understanding internally of what it wants to be famous for?	
3	If we spoke with your clients would they confirm what you are known for?	
4	Does your business have a clear point of differentiation from the competition?	
5	Overall do you feel your business has a consistently clear position in the market?	

Positioning is the foundation of revenue generating activity – get this right and everything else will fall into place much more easily because you have a focus for all your marketing decisions and all your interactions with customers, staff and suppliers. Ryanair and Emirates have both got strong, if radically different, positioning. You know what to expect when dealing with them both. An IT service provider we were working with did some detailed work on their positioning and discovered that when clients visited their offices all the good work they had done building their friendly reputation was undone (the offices were in a really seedy part of town!). It may not sound like "marketing", but moving office made a noticeable difference to their revenue growth.

Capability – does your business have a functional marketing resource and a marketing budget?

		✓, – or ✗
1	Do you have the right level of marketing skills and experience in your business?	
2	Does your marketing team have a clear structure (into the board and down the line)?	
3	Does your marketing team have an understanding of what the business issues/targets are for the next 12 months? And are results being measured?	
4	Does your marketing and business development team have all the tools it needs to do the job (e.g., databases, CRM systems etc.)?	
5	Do you have a marketing budget and has it been set to a financial formula?	

This section is about your 'marketing engine room' – the people, functional structures and processes, budgets and other resources (such as databases) that you need to power your marketing and business development. More than one business owner we know has said, "I would just like to fix things so that I can go and spend three months on the beach." Looked at another way, your business is less attractive to a buyer if all the revenue generation is down to you.

Channel – do you know which channels give you access to your clients?

		✓ , – or ✗
1	Do you understand the most effective channels that supply business to your company (these could be marketing channels or partner relationships)?	
2	Do you regularly measure the effectiveness of your channels/partners?	
3	Did you actively choose/seek those channels?	
4	Are you convinced your current channels are the most effective for your business?	
5	Do you have clear and planned programmes for each of your channels/partners that include communication and service?	

Here you should be thinking about how you source new business. Or, looked at another way, how new clients find you. Examples might include direct sales activity or third party referrals or the internet. Your firm's ability to open new channels is one of the key things that will make you more attractive to prospective buyers of your business. The IT business mentioned earlier took this approach and found that a supplier they used to do work for on Apple systems soon became a solid introducer of new clients with Microsoft issues.

Buyer's Journey – what makes them buy from you?

		✓, – or ✗
1	Do you know how your clients currently buy from you?	
2	Are you aware of how many touches (points of contact) you have with clients before they purchase from your business?	
3	Is your marketing/communication activity supporting the buying process of your clients?	
4	Have you asked your clients how and why they buy from your business?	
5	Do you understand why they buy from you rather than your competitors and vice versa?	

This box is all about understanding what makes your clients and customers tick – and ultimately buy from you. If you understand that, you are then in a better position to influence them more effectively and convert more leads into revenue. We are constantly surprised at the number of businesses that throw money at marketing initiatives ranging from CRM implementation to social media platforms without spending any money or time talking to clients and prospects to find out what they really want. Perhaps this is a reflection of the number of marketing agencies knocking on doors selling the latest shiny thing. For example, most of our clients worry about search engine optimisation (SEO), largely because they get lots of approaches from specialist agencies trying to convince them they should spend thousands on this technique. For some of them, it's the right thing to do, but for others who will always get work primarily through word of mouth there are better ways to use digital marketing to support their offline channels.

Communication – understanding the language of your business

		✓, – or ✗
1	Does your communication encourage the right interaction with clients, prospective clients and other stakeholders?	
2	Do you have clear and consistent branding, language pattern and tone of voice?	
3	Do your customers understand the benefits of working with your business?	

4	Does your communication build interest and a desire to act?	
5	Are you using the right media to reach your target audiences?	

Traditionally this is where most small businesses make the most mistakes in marketing. Many see marketing as synonymous with communications and leap in without any clear idea of, for example, their positioning or their buyers' journeys. Others forget that communication involves listening as well as speaking and opt for the marketing equivalent of shouting loudly at the passing crowds. Does it work for end-of-the-world doomsayers with their sandwich boards? Does it work for business? Professional marketers and marketing agencies are traditionally strong in this area and these are some of the questions they ask themselves.

Starting Conversations – measuring sales and performance

		✓, – or ✗
1	Do you have a structured sales department?	
2	Do your sales and marketing teams work together?	
3	Do they all have clarity on where the sales focus needs to be directed?	
4	Do you have a clear sales process?	
5	Are sales measured and reported on frequently enough?	

In this box we want you to be thinking about how you generate leads, and the processes you have in place to nurture and convert them, and measure effectiveness. A sizeable commercial roofing contractor was having problems with their revenue growth and a lot of heat was focussed on the sales team. Changing the language was a key part of dealing with this. Using "sales" as the key word meant there was a lot of emotion and ego in meetings and no progress was made. Focussing on the overall revenue, capability and reputation problem (using the Nine Box Matrix) led to the business having calmer discussions about how they "started conversations" with prospects and identifying that the sales team's roles had changed over the years to include more client management, leaving them less time to start new conversations. From there it was a small step for us to help them appoint a good telemarketing agency to fill the gap.

Product /Service – what are they buying?

		✓ , – or ✗
1	Do you measure yourself against your competitors' offerings?	
2	Are your products/services aligned with your position?	
3	Does your business often review what you put out into the market place?	
4	Do you have a product development team?	
5	Are you still selling the same products/services packaged in the same way as you did before the recession?	

Again this is one of the foundations of your revenue-generating activity and needs to be kept under regular review to keep up with changing market conditions and competitive activity. Ask yourself not just 'what are we selling?' but also 'what are our clients buying?' The answers may be different! Possibly the most pertinent lesson of recent years is that it's unlikely your customers are buying the same thing in a protracted recession as they were in the far distant boom. (And by the same token, they are unlikely to buy what you are shaping now when the economy and their confidence turns.) One example of this you may know well. There was a day when businesses chose different suppliers for different PC needs. Such as buying WordPerfect for what was called "word processing", Lotus 123 for spreadsheet work and Harvard Graphics for presentations. Then Microsoft packaged them all on one CD and called it Office. Which do you use now?

Client Management – do you know who your clients really are?

		✓, − or ✗
1	Can you easily get client information including billings and profit from your systems (whether you call it a CRM system, a practice management system or whatever)?	
2	Does your business have defined client criteria – which are the good and bad clients?	
3	Do you carry out regular reviews of your key client relationships and produce *written* plans for how you are going to develop those relationships?	

4	Do you actively choose not to work with some clients/prospects?	
5	Do you have a defined client management function that understands and guides the sales strategy?	

This is all about segmenting your client/customer base and making sure that each segment gets what it wants while still making you a profit. It's about avoiding that all-too-common situation where you can point to those clients who always seem to take up a disproportionate amount of your time and energy and which you know, in truth, probably cost you more than they pay. We did this exercise with one law firm and, lo-and-behold, 20% of their client base did generate 80% of their profits. Conversely, you may imagine how they felt when they looked at the red numbers representing the profits generated by the bottom 20% or so. A financial advisor business we did this exercise with rapidly found a competitor with a different positioning and business model who was able to service this bottom segment profitably – and sold this part of the business to them.

Client Service – are your client service levels aligned?

		✓, – or ✗
1	Do you have someone responsible for managing the client service programme?	
2	Are you consciously under-servicing and/or over-servicing clients?	
3	Do you have a structured client service programme?	

4	Do you know how many products/services your clients buy from you?	
5	Do you regularly carry out research to understand client satisfaction levels and their perceptions of your business?	

This area is closely linked to Client Management and looks at the activities you undertake to service your different client segments to ensure high levels of satisfaction, repeat business and referral. The key to good service is to think about the energy in the relationship your customer has with you. This doesn't always go the way you thought. In the world of cycling, a habit seems to have evolved across the board of enclosing small packs of Haribos with online orders (for non-cyclist readers, these go down well as a treat on any ride!). When customers first receive these they generate a lot of positive word of mouth with fellow cyclists: "You'll never guess what I got when I bought those brake pads from ABC Co." When everyone has been doing it for a while, it is not only no longer something you tell your mates about on a ride, it tends to reverse: "Guess what, I bought some new tyres from XYZ Co and they didn't even send me any Haribo." You laugh, but how do you feel when one of your main suppliers no longer invites you to the races – or even stops giving you those fancy pads of paper you used to like passing on to your kids?

Seeing the bigger picture

Now, let's pull your reflections together to see the bigger picture using the Nine Box Matrix.

FIND	CONVERT	DELIVER
POSITION	BUYERS JOURNEY	PRODUCT / SERVICES
CAPABILITY	COMMUNI-CATION	CLIENT MANAGEMENT
CHANNEL	STARTING CONVERSATIONS	CLIENT SERVICE

Look at the answers to the five questions in each section and then score yourself for each box as follows:

- Give yourself two points if it's all sorted and working well
- Give yourself one point if it's working OK – it could be better but it's not a major concern
- Give yourself zero points if it's not working well at all and it's keeping you awake at night

What your results tell you and what you need to do next

First, let's take a look at your overall score.

0–30 points: Your marketing is a bit of a Damp Squib – you're either not sure what to do and/or you're not doing it very well.

31–60 points: You are Dabbling in marketing – some of it's OK but there's definitely room for improvement.

61–90 points: Dynamite! It sounds as though you are both clear on what to do and making it happen, but it may be worth looking carefully at potential weak spots.

Now look at the areas you score lowest in – in which sections did you score lowest? These are probably the areas to focus on first but that will depend on your business and where it is in its life-cycle.

What do we mean by this? Let's look at how you scored in the three different areas of Finding, Converting and Delivering. Which was your weakest area? And contrast that with which matters most to your business at present.

For example, a start-up business may score lowest on Delivering but that might not matter if the priority is to identify target markets, develop a proposition and get out and build a client base. As long as they are scoring well on Finding and Converting, they may be OK for now.

Conversely, a mature business with a substantial base of existing clients might score poorly on some of the areas of Converting new business, but that might be relatively unimportant compared to low scores for Delivery, given that they would expect the majority of their revenue to come from repeat business or referrals.

For this reason, when we do this exercise in practice we return to it regularly as the business evolves and its priorities change.

> "When did you last get your clients' views on what you do?"

Don't spread yourself too thinly

The key to what to do next is

- Identify what matters to your business
- Be clear on where your most important weak spots are
- Pick no more than three to focus on – be realistic about what you can achieve and don't spread your resources too thinly.

With these priorities clear in your mind for 'what' to do, now you can get on with developing a focused marketing plan, and make clear choices about which activities are essential.

So how does this work in practice?

This way of looking at marketing has been used now by a number of entrepreneurial firms to put some real focus in their strategy and help them concentrate on activities that will make a difference. It's been used in businesses as diverse as technology companies, commercial builders, engineering and manufacturing firms and professional services like law and accounting. So how does it work in practice?

The start point is usually to get the key decision makers in the business together to set marketing priorities. Everyone always has a view on what marketing works, so agreement is often no mean feat in itself. Running a facilitated prioritisation workshop around the 9 box tool works in two ways: it makes sure the conversations are about 'what the business needs to do', not 'how do we do it?', and it allows everyone to have their say while ensuring no one pet project dominates.

In about half of the cases mentioned above, research was also done to establish what the clients and customers thought about the business. This brought the all-important Buyers' Journey into the equation – and a neutral viewpoint not aligned with any particular decision maker. When was the last time you actively sought your buyers' (and even staff and suppliers') views on what you offer?

At the end of the workshop the business usually has agreement on what the key marketing priorities are and how they support the revenue and cultural aims of the firm. For example, one of the engineering firms mentioned above realised that they had defined a good position in the market place, but it wasn't really embedded in the way they did things, so they weren't benefiting from it commercially. Their marketing priorities became to improve Communications, create a Client Management process and open new Channels to market. In the case of Client Management, for example, this led to the creation of a process for segmenting the client base, the creation of templates for client plans and coaching of the client teams to develop those plans. Similar strategies and implementation options were identified for their communications and new channel programmes.

Section 3

How do I make it all happen and who can I get to help?

"Marketing" is a horribly fuzzy word, which is why we suggest focusing on the aspects of marketing that matter to business owners: growing Revenue, having the Capability to do things well (and repeatedly) and managing Reputation. To get this sort of marketing function and culture working well in a business the owner or CEO is going to have to ensure a number of things happen.

Such as:

- Creating a realistic marketing and business development plan
- Working out how much to budget, and on what
- Getting the right skills and resources for implementation
- Turning good intentions into action – not just once but on an ongoing basis
- Measuring effectiveness and the return on your investment

Rather than take you through the detail of these tasks, we're going to suggest that as an established owner of a successful business you shouldn't be doing any of them yourself, as that's not your role. Even if you have a marketing background, as CEO or owner you need to ask yourself if it's what the business really needs for you to be immersed in the 'how' of implementation. And whether you need to get some specialist expertise to turn your strategy into action.

What are my choices?

Agencies

To grow your revenue you'll work with a wide range of marketing agencies. Ad agencies, web agencies, PR agencies, research agencies, even list brokers, telesales and CRM agencies. Decide if you want them as a long term member of your team and whether they can provide the creative spark that gets your messages across, as well as being good deliverers.

It is vital to remember an agency is only as good as the brief you give them. How good are your marketing agency briefing skills?

Freelancers

If you know what you want, it's often quickest and most cost efficient to find, for example, a copy writer who knows your industry or a telesales freelancer who wants a few more days' regular work with a business they like. You can even make use of freelance marketing execs to fill gaps in your team for specific projects. The trick with freelancers, after finding them, is to manage them well.

Marketing staff

For SMEs creating a revenue generating team, it is often difficult to know exactly what you want out of a permanent marketing hire, especially if you are creating or restructuring the marketing function in the business. How to decide the best course of action here is, unfortunately, outside the scope of this chapter.

In-house or outsourced partner?

More and more senior roles are being performed by outsourced directors until such time as the business can afford a permanent member of staff and their team. Consider whether now is the right time to get a permanent marketing and revenue generating director on board, or whether you would benefit from partnering for this role too.

What do I want the team to do?

We have developed a decision making tool that works on two levels: gut feel and detailed thinking. Start by thinking about the high level functions that your business needs:

Vision: Your money will be wasted if you don't have someone who shares your vision of what marketing can achieve for your business.

Strategy: Who's going to work out *what* you need to do in the business in order to be good at marketing, i.e., growing revenue, capability and reputation?

Implementation: Some of these tasks will be internally-focused, like coordinating sales and marketing or working with directors. Others will be externally-focused, like building websites, conducting detailed market research or lobbying journalists.

Mentoring: You will want someone in the team who is able to see beyond the current project and think about who's going to do it next time and how you can prepare them for it.

You may also want to add in parameters that are important for your business. Some examples could be:

Implementation neutrality: Would you ask a web design agency that employs coders and graphic designers whether you should be spending less on your website and more on researching what customers want?

Flexibility: These days good competitive marketing outside the world of large corporates requires trying lots of new things and testing how, if at all, to make them work for you. You need to be able to turn taps on and off. Can you?

Assembling a team

This is an example worked through with the CEO of an accounting firm. These are the people who he was used to talking to about marketing matters. (It's at the next stage that you can go on to create a more detailed version breaking the main headings into their sub-parts e.g., "implementation" into writing copy, database entry, organising events etc.).

Trusting your gut instinct, you now need to go down each column to either tick or cross the boxes to indicate whom you believe can really help with each part. This is how the CEO saw things when we started work with the firm:

	Myself (CEO)	Partners	Web agency	PR agency
Vision	✓	✓	✗	✗
Strategy	✓	?	✗	?
Execution	✗	✓/✗	✓	✓
Mentoring	✗	✗	✗	✗
Neutral			✗	✗
Flexible			✓	✓

The CEO felt alone in formulating strategy. His partners all had opinions, but they varied and weren't informed by marketing expertise or best practice. He also felt there was a gap between those in the firm who did come up with strategy and those who implemented marketing activities (evidenced by phrases like "they just don't get it" and "why does our marketing feel so disjointed?"). The agencies the firm used were fine, but weren't able to help the CEO take an across-the-board strategic view of what they needed to do to meet their revenue targets.

If you do this for your business, what does it tell you about who you need to have working on your marketing?

Case study: Multiple office accountancy firm with 10+ partners

The CEO and accounting firm we are talking about, although weathering the recession successfully, was looking to grow its fee income by around 16 per cent while extending its positioning as all-round business advisors. The partners knew they should be doing more proactive marketing if they were to achieve their financial goals, and they also felt the time had come to invest in a marketing function for the first time, but they were unsure as to what level of person to recruit.

The firm also wanted to move fast, so RCR stepped into the breach and acted as the firm's hands-on marketing director for a few months, working on projects two days a week. Some of this involved acting as a strategic advisor to the CEO, helping tie priorities to financial objectives. Some of it involved the day-to-day legwork that marketing small businesses requires.

The CEO finally had the make-up of marketing team he wanted to ensure that the right activities were chosen and done:

	Myself (CEO)	Partners	Outsourced Marketing Director	Full Time Marketing Manager	Web agency	PR agency
Vision	✓	✓	✓	✗	✗	✗
Strategy	✓	?	✓	?	✗	?
Execution	✗	✓/✗	✓	✓	✓	✓
Mentoring	✗	✗	✓	✗	✗	✗
Neutral		✗	✓	✓	✗	✗
Flexible		n/a	✓	✗	✓	✓

While working in the business we then fleshed out a detailed spec of who would do each marketing job and this helped identify the right sort of marketing manager to recruit. That person is now in place managing agencies and day-to-day marketing activities and working with the RCR outsourced marketing director, who provides strategic guidance and mentoring and is called in for special projects like opening up new markets.

Over the year following the adoption of the marketing strategy, RCR and the accounting firm have been monitoring a range of indicators to track progress, such as numbers of mailings, digital activity and increased numbers of formal client plans. The key measure, particularly in convincing the partners that a marketing function is a good investment, has been the firm's increase in revenues to hit the targets set for the year.

Making the first move

Growing your business to the next level usually requires doing something different. That's why we've done three things in this chapter:

- Shared the **mindset** of those running successful businesses. Continually asking yourself "why" bother with marketing – and coming back to how good marketing will make your business more valuable to a potential buyer

- Looked at **decision making** and shared a tool that you can use to make sure you've got focus in your marketing and are not getting distracted by the latest shiny thing

- Discussed assembling a **team** that will reliably get the marketing done for you.

If this has rung any bells with you, all we can do now is urge you to take the first steps to boosting your company's marketing. The tools and exercises we have described make a good start – give them a try and see if they give you the insights you need to decide what to do next.

You can keep your mind on marketing matters by following our regular reflections on growing your revenue at www.rcrpartnership.com/follow

And a final word of advice – don't forget to carry out regular progress reviews of results and plans. This isn't a once-and-forever process!

Alan says:

Most smaller companies engage in marketing and sales activity with the absolute enthusiasm of those who are excited about their new product/service and know clearly who they should be selling to.

They have a clear understanding of their competitive advantage and sweep all before them. As the company grows, however, and roles expand and functions divide, the focus and responsibility for customers become much narrower.

The marketing mindset that once the whole company possessed is diminished as delivery, administration and finance take equal importance.

Victoria and Paul are arguing in this chapter that a better organised and focused marketing approach, driven by a well staffed and directed marketing team, will help you to move up a level in company performance.

Part of that process is for the marketing function to help all staff recognise the importance of the customer to ensure that all client contact with the company is seen as a high quality experience.

Successful companies tend to focus on coordination between all functions, managers, specialist expertise and strategies in such a way that customers cannot see the joins. An effective marketing organisation can help you as CEO to achieve this goal, which is proven to improve the bottom line on a sustainable basis.

MAKE TECHNOLOGY WORK FOR YOU

Avoid Costly ICT Mistakes

Shakeeb Niazi

How do you get technology to work for you and help achieve your business objectives rather than being seen as just another cost to the business?

Make Technology Work For You

Making technology work for you and avoiding costly mistakes – now there's a challenge! Technology is often seen as an expensive burden, but with the right planning and application it can help you achieve your business objectives.

For some businesses, technology has become an integral part of their success. Organisations such as banks and retailers, for example, rely almost entirely on technology for their efficient operation and give it due consideration in their business planning.

Many other organisations, however, have found that ICT (Information and Communications Technology) has been forced upon them and it has thus been adopted reluctantly, or on a piecemeal basis. This reactive approach means that the focus is on problem-solving rather than business objectives; which in turn means that business advantages which could be derived from things such as improved websites and search engine optimisation become an afterthought.

This significantly inhibits the effectiveness of future investment and can force major upheavals in systems to bring them up to date; something that usually has to occur when these procedures are least expected or wanted.

An integrated approach is vital to business success, and will lead to an improvement in both organisational processes and profits. Through case studies I hope to demonstrate not only the steps involved in the process of acquiring, developing and upgrading the relevant systems, but also how important it is to get into the mind-set that appropriate technology is an essential component of profitability.

You will see that all the case studies begin with an ICT Health Check, which is something that you should consider doing for your own business. This evaluates not only a company's current business objectives, ICT systems and the problems they face, but also takes a strategic overview of where the company hopes to be in five years and how technology could help them get there. It's an important tool, both for planning technology investment and business growth, as it forces you to firm up your ideas, set objectives and confront issues that you may have previously swept under the carpet.

In our ICT Health Checks we always put a lot of emphasis on a company's potential future development so that a phased programme of technological enhancements can be considered, even if it is not appropriate to implement it at the early stage. Future-proofing our proposals is not always possible, but considering all of the options is part of the integrated approach I have already emphasised and helps to balance the short term priority outcomes – for example, increased sales leads from the website – with longer-term requirements both potential and actual.

CASE STUDIES

The following are two example case studies, looking at companies of differing sizes and sectors to help illustrate how technology can change – and in some cases save, a business.

I have chosen these case studies as they reflect how technology can resolve business issues, regardless of the size or composition of a company. These also help us illustrate growth, scalability and transition requirements that can easily be met as organisations grow and their needs change.

We often find that our clients' challenges are much the same in technological terms. For example, all companies need a secure ICT infrastructure (computers, networks and telecoms) but this needs to be tailored in varying ways according to budget, location and their specific business needs.

Our first case study is of a small scale accountancy business whose owner had significant ambitions for growth.

Company Profile - ABC Accountants Ltd

Sector:	Business to Business - accounts, bookkeeping and payroll services for small-medium enterprises (<£1m)
Size:	4 part-time employees
ICT:	5 laptops using a wireless network to connect to a PC in the corner acting as a server
APPS:	Quick Books, Sage Accounting, MS Office
Background:	John, a qualified accountant, was made redundant from his job and was forced to become self-employed by the current market environment. He ended up taking bookkeeping jobs to make ends meet. After about a year working from home, he started to take on new employees part-time, to minimise costs. Three years on, the business has grown to 4 part-time employees. John now has a small office and is working 7 days a week. He feels that he cannot develop the business as he does not have the time. If he gains a new customer, for example, he cannot adequately service their needs - yet he cannot pass responsibilities to his staff as they leave when they get a full-time job offer. Cash-flow is the main problem: John's business model is to do the work and charge the customers after delivery. He also allows time for customers to review the books and then pay. But the customers are small and rarely check the paperwork, and - worse still - very rarely pay on time. John also feels he cannot increase prices as he cannot afford to lose any customers, even though costs have increased since he leased his office. As a result, his profit margin is under pressure and decreasing.

We were called in to advise John on how technology could be a cost-effective way of solving his business problems, and the process is documented below. You will see how an integrated approach can benefit a business, as well as the importance of treating ICT as a viable tool for business growth rather than just another expense.

Step 1. ICTHC & DRD – ICT Health Check and Disaster Recovery Documentation

We started by undertaking an ICT Health Check (investigation phase), which included a hardware and software inventory, as well as recording hardware warranties and the number of licenses in use. Remember that these all affect your costs!

When you run a Health Check on your own business, it is also very important to include any digital assets you may have, such as your internet domains and web hosting accounts. Make a catalogue of these, along with the user names and passwords, and store them in a secure password-protected document. This is the start of your Disaster Recovery documentation.

Pay particular attention to ownership and registration details of domain names – these are extremely valuable, so why are they registered in your secretary's/web developer's/IT director's name? They will be in the 'power seat' in any dispute!

We are constantly being asked to retrieve domains from ex- or disgruntled employees, which can be a costly exercise. It is good business sense to take personal ownership of your domains.

The findings in the ICT Health Check will help you plan your ICT consolidation, ensure that everything is working correctly and remain operational. Document the infrastructure and start planning what the business needs for future growth. Don't buy, but plan.

Step 2. GA & P4G – Gap Analysis and Planning for Growth

We then documented all of ABC's existing revenue-generating activities that had an ICT element (e.g. lead generation) and mapped out what they wanted in future. This allowed us to conduct a 'gap analysis', or in other words to work out where they were and where they wanted to be. This gave us a clear direction and set of goals that we could work towards.

For example, ABC had a website, but it had failed to generate a single sales lead over the two years it had been live. Before we redesigned the website we did some research. It was important to understand:

•   Who was their ideal customer?

•   Where were they located?

•   How did they (the potential customers) make decisions to buy?

We used their existing customer base as the survey starting point, which gave us a specific picture of their ideal customer. We then started considering the design, the copy and search engine optimisation (SEO) – this is the process of optimising how a 'search engine' like Google understands what your website is about. The process involves using key words and key phrases which help Google index your website. This ensures that people can find you when they search for your type of service.

Search Engine Optimisation is absolutely vital to any successful website. Your web developer should be SEO savvy and plan this aspect from the very beginning, otherwise you will be forever making changes – and paying for extra man hours – before it goes live.

Step 3. GL2CS – Generate Leads To Create Sales

We agreed with ABC that the primary goal of the website should be increasing lead generation, but we were also aware that generating lots of worthless enquires can damage a business, as can not having the resources in place to contact the customers in a timely manner.

You can largely avoid these issues through the text you include on your website. Part of the website copy's responsibility is to help prequalify the lead, so the contact form should ask where they are and what timeframe they are working to – this allows you to weed out clients that it will be impossible to service.

Additionally, you can set up a prequalifying process whereby you call the lead with your sales information at the ready, then as part of the conversation gather the same type of information as the feedback form example above. These are now called 'pre-qualified leads' and you should manage these leads by setting priorities against them based on whether they are likely to buy and when. If you then follow-up with each pre-qualified lead based on the priority you have assigned to them, you automatically have the basis of a sales pipeline.

It may seem out of sequence but you need to make sure your sales pipeline is working before you start to generate more leads; otherwise you are just wasting your resources. Remember that the overall aim is to generate leads and convert to sales which will provide you with additional income, improved cash-flow, increased profitability and a much larger customer base.

For ABC, the new website was built over a couple of months and launched in September. The customer research and planning had clearly paid off:

- There was a dramatic increase in leads: the first one came only two months after the website re-launch, the second came the following month and four came the month after. The website now generates an average of two leads per week

- Prequalifying measures created only high-quality leads and the conversion rate averaged over 80%

- The company had a higher local profile (it appeared more regularly in local searches and word of mouth began to spread)

The website was quickly acknowledged as an integral part of ABC's business development strategy. It was able to be such a successful part of business growth because, whilst we added to the complexity of the website solution, we made sure we did not increase the burden of maintenance or the cost to ABC.

Step 4. GTPR – Get the Price Right: Increase Your Prices

Once new client acquisition had been simplified, ABC was ready to start taking a more holistic view of their business model and strategy.

After a short workshop on business modelling and pricing, ABC agreed that their prices should be increased by 20%. They were, however, concerned that they would lose their existing customers, even those that were late payers. So they allowed their existing customers to continue with the existing prices, as long as the customers started paying monthly by standing order. This ensured that the service did not cost the existing customers any more, but that they started to pay regularly in advance of any work carried out. Customers who did not want to do this simply paid more.

The cash-flow position soon changed from negative to positive for the first time. All new customers were encouraged to take up monthly pre-payment on the new pricelist. After three months they were in a position to approach the late paying customers and renegotiate the charges.

The key benefit of this strategy is to stop delays in receiving income, which improves cashflow and therefore profitability. It is worth sitting down and mapping out how you might remodel your own business proposition.

Step 5. IINI & USTS – Invest in Infrastructure and Use Skilled Technical Support

Over time the positive cash-flow enabled ABC to replace all their desktop PCs, upgrade the main server to an SBS (small business server), add online backups and include electronic faxing. Suddenly they had a new, greatly improved, ICT system!

Simply getting customers to pay more quickly was not sufficient to achieve all these changes, but by using our technology leasehold and rental agreements ABC greatly improved their cash flow without compromising on the service they acquired. Additionally, by using our skilled ICT support service, internal staff were relieved of any ICT responsibility and free to concentrate on their work – making the business more profitable.

Apart from the reduction in capital ICT expenditure, we were able to bring about significant improvements in performance and the reliability of the computer systems. We were also able to include a disaster recovery facility.

Step 6. MPC – Make Positive Changes

The next stage was to divide the team by responsibility.

An employee was promoted to full-time team leader for the majority of the part-time staff and smaller customers. Even though they were employed full-time, they continued to work a couple of days from home. To overcome this issue we installed a fast PC and a secure link from their home back to the office. Having a 'connected system' added to the stability and continuity of the bookkeeping work. Whether employees were in the office or at home the systems worked the same way. We also spent some time training the staff to improve both their PC skills and their workplace ICT accountabilities.

As a result they took responsibility for their data and established appropriate backup policies and procedures, which sat alongside the new disaster recovery processes that were introduced as part of the upgrade. This included, for example, what actions to take if a customer's bookkeeping database became corrupt. We also trained individual employees in specialist tasks so that they could become the 'go to' person for a technology or process problem, facilitating the work of their colleagues.

Over time, the new formal processes and structure within the team kept staff engaged, and they were motivated by the major positive change they saw happening. You will be surprised how a fast PC uplifts morale and how fast a slow PC diminishes it!

Synopsis

Our client was overwhelmed with work and by a cash flow problem, which he was convinced would not allow him to invest in his business – especially not in new ICT. He had no time to prospect for new business and, as our initial investigation showed, his website was not generating any new leads. Many of the basic housekeeping issues essential for a well-managed ICT system were also not in place.

Whilst we have used an accountants firm in the case study, this applies to all time-based businesses where the owner is squeezed between accumulating charge-out hours and managing the business. These include businesses such as bookkeepers, solicitors, temporary staff agencies and in fact any small professional practice.

For ABC, we were able to highlight the fact that improvements to the operational procedures of the company could facilitate a new pricing policy, that an SEO-enabled website would generate new leads and that a rental agreement for the provision of the ICT equipment would remove the need for capital investment. These helped ABC achieve a balance of investment and income generation, and key results were:

- The new pricing policy and monthly pre-payment model improved margins as well as cashflow

- A rental agreement for the new equipment reduced capital outlay and to an extent future-proofed the system, contingent on the growth of the company and the advance of technology

- Staff were happier with clearer responsibilities and employee turnover significantly reduced over time. As a result workload was more efficiently delegated and the owner has more time at home, especially at weekends

- New leads came in regularly and, with the advantage of a fully functioning ICT system, the leads were more readily converted to sales and retained. Much of the client contact was maintained online, reducing the flow of paper and improving customer service.

We are now in discussion with the client as to how the business model can be franchised nationwide.

Key things to consider:

- Do you have a disaster recovery plan?
- Where should your business be in 5 years, and how can technology help you get there?
- Does your current website generate enough high-quality leads?
- Have you planned your SEO?
- Are your ICT systems set up to facilitate client management?
- Does your ICT infrastructure support your business?
- Is your business model viable?
- Are your staff engaged, and confident in using your ICT systems?

Company Profile - XYZ Stationery Online Ltd

Sector:	Business to Business - Stationery and Office products and services to medium enterprises (<£20m)
Size:	10 office employees, 20 drivers and 5 warehouse staff
ICT:	10 PCs, 4 laptops using a wireless network to connect to a server in the server room
APPS:	E-commerce website
Background:	David, a salesman by trade, set up his business 25 years ago when he decided to marry and start a family. His sales job selling business equipment allowed him to meet many businesses and get to know the decision makers. He quickly realised that supplying stationery and other office consumables was highly profitable if sold as a service and on account. He quickly set up a mail-order and telephone ordering service (relatively new at the time) and bought his first van. The business has grown considerably but the market has changed; he has a small office and a large warehouse and to grow sales he has to employ more staff. He feels that he needs to develop the business but the costs of using mail-order catalogues is increasing, so he has decided to invest in a website. Current ICT Systems supported on an as-needed basis. No formal ICT processes are in place.

In our second case study we look more closely at the importance of designing an appropriate, SEO-enhanced website and the benefits of including relevant technology to ensure that it perfectly fits the needs of a business. After reading this, consider conducting a review of your own website – try seeing it from an outsider's perspective, and evaluate its strengths and weaknesses in an honest manner. You might be surprised by what you come up with!

Step 1. ICTHC & DRD – ICT Health Check and Disaster Recovery Documentation

We started by undertaking an ICT Health Check. For this client we recorded details of all their ICT suppliers, along with the services they were supplying and the amount they charged. We also recorded all the contract cancellation terms – when you engage any new supplier pay particular attention to the stipulated notice period and any penalties that could be enforced.

We also carried out a full business analysis of the website requirements and decided that an e-commerce website solution was appropriate. Instead of using the website as just a catalogue to replace the one in print, we designed a solution that was part catalogue and part e-commerce shop so that customers could order directly online. This allowed us to focus the SEO on the catalogue section which rarely changed, meaning that we could write SEO-friendly copy.

Step 2. BDP – Business Development Plan

The findings in the ICT Health Check helped identify the key ICT services that they needed. Using this information we formulated a 'business transformation plan' that covered changes to their ICT, a new e-commerce solution and the impact on their processes.

One key transformation we realised was necessary was related to the order management system. Their existing system was not web-enabled, and although many people would have said that this was a problem, we considered it a vital business opportunity. We realised that we could design specific 'gateways' that allowed us to perform many tasks in real-time, rather than relying on the traditional once-a-day upload of prices and product availability or download of sales information. For example, as prices changed on their local order management system, these updated prices could be synchronised with the website.

Step 3. GTPR – Get the Price Right: Create Customer Centric Pricing

We thus designed the e-commerce website to constantly check prices from the local order management system. This meant that the price of every item was confirmed, but the overhead from doing so was minimal compared to the traditional method. The added benefit was that the company could now cope with complex customer-centric pricing, meaning that every customer had their own agreed price list. XYZ could reduce the prices on frequently purchased items and uplift the cost for others. This actually resulted in a substantial increase in their profit margins.

Step 4. GL2CS – Generate Leads To Create Sales

We also carried out a similar exercise when we captured new sales on the website. We saved the data on a hosted server like other traditional solutions, but at the same time we created the order on their local order management system, which meant the order could be processed almost immediately. You will have noticed that some online shops have a cut-off time. They say something like 'order before 3pm for next day delivery'. The system we designed meant that the vans could be loaded in the evening for the next day, but just before they left at 7am in the morning the overnight orders could also be added.

Results

Following our analysis and planning we designed an SEO-enhanced e-commerce website to bring in new customers and facilitate sales processes, providing additional income and improved cashflow. The build took three months but results were almost instantaneous:

- There was a dramatic increase in sales; with the first one coming only hours after the website was launched. By the second week over 50% of the sales were coming through the website, a figure which had risen to 70% by the end of the month

- The company grew its London-wide profile thanks to SEO and increased customer satisfaction.

The website now forms an integral part of XYZ's business development strategy. The integrated structure of the website means that making changes and upgrades is easy and that it does not impact on the company's day-to-day business. The website has paid for itself many times over and maintenance and support are cost effective.

Synopsis

An open-minded approach to sales technology can deliver huge benefits. In this instance, a remodelled business proposition whereby customer-centric pricing played a large role in online sales had a huge impact on XYZ's profits. Keen pricing could be negotiated on their frequently purchased items, whilst others bought less often were priced with a substantial level of margin. As the customers changed their buying habits they did not re-negotiate their prices. This resulted in a substantial increase in XYZ's profit margin. The overall result was an uplift in the average order value, improving cashflow and margin.

Once this was in place, we were also able to address the issues related to the costly ICT suppliers we had identified in the Health Check. With the introduction of a rental agreement we were able to replace all the desktop PCs and upgrade the main servers, add online backups and electronic faxing and deliver a greatly improved ICT system. The new ICT system and the new e-commerce solution removed the need for most of the ICT suppliers, which we consolidated down to just one after six months. This improved the cost-effectiveness of the system and ensured that support was always available in case something went wrong.

Overall, this demonstrates how our investigative approach can help a business focus on what they really need, rather than what they think they need. A great deal of trust has to be gained for such a major change in the business to occur, but once it has been achieved business and ICT teams can engage in building a positive business model.

The results were:

- Improved cash flow and sales from an altered business model

- Increased numbers of new customers from their new lead-generating e-commerce website solution

- Transformed business model from an old fashioned telesales/catalogue business to an online business

- Switched ICT model to a rental model to assist in the company's growth.

Future Steps

The next stage is to build e-commerce solutions for specific markets, using the same core engine to drive the business forward. We have found that you can gain a more significant market share in new (but related) markets than you can in your own current market.

Key things to consider:

- Is your e-commerce solution facilitating sales?

- Can you easily update your prices and create individual price lists for customers?

- Do you know the terms under which your current ICT contracts are based?

- Could you benefit from an innovative look at your business model?

- Can technology play a greater role in your business growth?

The basics of specifying a new ICT system and the five key areas of concern

Now that we have seen how investment in appropriate technology can benefit businesses, and how intelligent planning and an open-minded approach can deliver growth, it's time to consider how companies can go about acquiring cost-effective, future-proof ICT systems that aid their business aims.

Few of us are prepared to risk running our business without any ICT systems. But there are still many who seem complacent enough to accept less than adequate systems and all the risks inherent in such a course of action.

By evaluating the five core questions businesses face when trying to commission ICT systems, we will learn about how to plan for a sustainable system that meets your business needs, and how to purchase the right technology.

1. The viability of component parts of your computer systems

We can all name various types of software and hardware, but it's important to understand how they fit together.

Information = Data, databases, documents and spreadsheets and any file containing data

Communication = Telephones, facsimiles, email, VOIP, websites and any medium presenting data

Technology = Servers, personal computers, modems, printers, network devices and any device holding or delivering data

As a business owner, you need to ask yourself whether all these assets are up to date, linked with one another and properly maintained. You also need to ensure that you have engineers on call should something go wrong.

Furthermore, you need to remember that ICT is an extremely fast-moving area of industry where – according to 'Moore's Law' – products double in capacity and halve in price every 18 months. This means you have to be constantly reviewing your position and the cost-effectiveness of your technology, a fact which applies to every business and not just those in ICT.

2. Potential loss of data and information

The information you have on your computer systems is the 'life-blood' of your business and any loss will have a negative effect on your productivity. It is thus essential that you protect your information – from accidents and from intruders.

Many businesses never fully recover from a data loss (i.e. server or PC failure where data cannot be easily recovered) because they lose vital information related to accounting, billing (especially payments due/outstanding), contracts and key employees. In the worst case scenario a company could go out of business, resulting in the loss of jobs and services to the marketplace.

We hear constantly of hackers breaking into major websites

and stealing, deleting or corrupting the data therein. Not only will your costs rise as a direct result of such an attack, but you could also experience a major loss in confidence within your marketplace, losing hard-won credentials and customers.

For example: 27th April 2011 – Sony confirmed the loss of personal information from its PlayStation Network (PSN) including name, address, email address and login details for PSN and Qriocity users, affecting around 77 million people – the cost of which has been estimated at £105 million. At the end of the financial year Sony posted record losses of $5.7 billion. (Source: Wikipedia)

The following selection of statistics illustrates the extent of the losses attributable to ICT systems and serves to highlight the need for full protection, if business owners wish to avoid the consequences of such a loss:

- **6% of all PCs will suffer an episode of data loss in any given year**

- **30% of all businesses that have a major fire go out of business within a year**

- **31% of PC users have lost all of their files due to events beyond their control**

- **34% of companies fail to test their tape backups, and of those that do, 77% have found tape back-up failures.**

3. How to avoid inadequate communication

Fast-moving new communication technologies such as VOIP are now available on mobiles, costs are falling thanks to global communications and remote working is increasing – ask any budding entrepreneur and they will describe their vision of working on a sunny beach and connecting to the office via their laptop with a cocktail in their hand.

The potential that these technologies create is endless, but how should you best go about using them to develop your business?

Simply define the things you need to do: include where you live (and where your key staff live), the distance to the office and consider the broadband connection that is available in both places. Will you be working from home or travelling widely?

Once you have a clearly defined a list of requirements, start talking to people around you and get some recommendations – don't forget there are plenty of software free trials. Those of you with access to skilled ICT professionals (not your nephew or any other relative who is always on his computer, but rather someone who makes their living from ICT) will find this easier.

4. Off the shelf packages vs. bespoke

Using off-the-shelf packages is great as they are designed to be easy to use, cheap to buy and cheap to maintain (some charge a yearly fee). The problems start when you want to integrate the packages; for example one provider might update their software and cause all your packages to stop working together. Indeed, integrating off the shelf packages can be costly and is not always guaranteed to succeed.

On the other hand, a bespoke system will reap benefits if delivered correctly. In fact, as entrepreneurs usually take a different approach to the market, perhaps because they have found a cheaper or more innovative way of delivering an existing product, or are introducing the world to something new, a generic solution can be a significant hindrance.

5. Purchasing the right kind of technology for your business

This is the costliest part of any ICT system and needs constant attention and replacement. The key things to remember are to make sure you have clear and up-to-date documents to cover your computer systems, and to make sure the system is robust and has been properly tested.

The key areas to think about when planning your business are:

- **Network Infrastructure**
Provision for expansion should have been made as part of the initial installation: for example to add a powerful firewall that does not need updating. Also being able to add extra, or even more powerful, network switches to improve bandwidth and to update the infrastructure without replacing network cables is essential.

With regards to cabling, always go for the highest spec cable such as Cat6 or Cat6a rather than Cat5. Remember that investing in good cable is ultimately cheaper than the labour and disruption costs you will incur if you have to reinstall cabling.

And don't use builders to install cable! They may be cheaper but it's a false economy: you end up paying for resulting issues such as pulled cable (the breakages caused in very thin copper cable if it's pulled too hard). Builders also tend to use the cheapest cable they can find, which causes network loss as well as slow networks. They also tend not to use fire resistant network cable – so if you have a fire your office will be full of toxic fumes.

- **PC and Server Infrastructure**

The PC and Server infrastructure should be simple as possible. Where you can, you should use identical equipment, which eases the problem of swapping of equipment when issues occur.

Whilst you don't have to worry about PC capacity, you should be aware that the file servers they communicate with do need to scale. In other words, the equipment you purchase should give you enough spare capacity to expand your business in the next 3-5 years. You might, for example, need to add more hard drives, so remember to purchase hardware with capacity that can be scaled as you grow.

Buy the best security you can afford: firewall, anti-virus, anti-intrusion detection and DNS protection. Buy an online backup service that has at least 256bit encryption, as well as compression from a company with ISO9001 certification along with a multitude of data silos in certified data centres adhering to ISO27001.

• **Peripherals**
The peripherals (extra devices connected by a cable) should be as simple as possible. Use identical equipment where possible, which eases the problems caused by swapping equipment when issues occur.

• **Applications**
These are software programs that run on your electronic devices.

Apps come in many different flavours. There are, for example, simple apps that you download and install to your mobile phones to tell you the time in another part of the world. Office apps such as Word, Excel and PowerPoint allow you to create documents, whilst server apps like Exchange and SharePoint allow you to collaborate. Then there are the Line-Of-Business (LOB) apps which are important to your business, but which you can live without for a day or two: for example Sage Accounting.

Finally, there are mission critical apps which are essential for your day-to-day business. A good example of this is an e-commerce website – if the website goes down the 'tills stop ringing'.

The key point to remember is about scalability. Office apps and any PC-based apps don't need to scale, unlike the server apps (such as mail and database servers) with which they communicate.

Conclusion: finding a technology partner, taking a positive attitude

Using the information from this chapter, you are now ready to evaluate your business's technology needs, have an informed conversation with a technology provider as to how ICT can facilitate your work, and work with them to secure strategic and forward-thinking solutions for your business.

When selecting a technology partner, don't be afraid to factor in the compatibility of your personalities, as you will need to work with the people you find for years. Make sure that they are professionals with a few years of experience and most importantly someone you can trust.

Ideally, before embarking on a bespoke system you should have already implemented and be working with off-the-shelf packages – this is to help you define the technical and functional requirements of the end system. You can also use this time to create a strategic approach to the evolution of your ICT by prioritising systems and subsystems based on development costs, return on investment and/or new business generation. Don't forget, for example, that investing in a new website has the potential to make you more money than buying a new colour printer that allows you to print your own leaflets.

Once you have a strategy, start looking around for a potential partner. It's usually best to start off with a generalist ICT supplier to look after your hardware, basic operating systems and office applications. Next, find yourself specialists in the area of those applications you wish to develop; finding one that covers more than one application could reap benefits in terms of costs and delivery times.

How do you go about identifying specialist firms? Companies, especially those in the ICT industry, don't actually advertise all their skills, so don't be afraid to ask questions. The best thing to do is to look for a company that will act as a delivery agent – in other words one which outsources some of the work. The advantages of doing this range from saving you time and money to transferring responsibility to a single point. This avoids a situation that many of us have been in, whereby things go wrong and one supplier then blames the other and vice-versa – the end client is always the loser.

Regardless of which supplier and what technology you choose to work with, the most important thing is to adopt a positive attitude towards what benefits adopting new technology can have for your business. In particular, it is vital to lead from the front and demonstrate the value of investing in technology to your employees. From the very beginning of your business educate everyone that 'change is good' and that you can always improve a process.

However, it's equally important that you don't make changes just because you can. Each change should be based on a business case where you calculate the return financially, by time or by improvement of customer experience - this is usually missed out of calculations.

Finally, everyone can buy the same equipment, source the same support services and use the same applications, so what is the key differentiator between businesses? Information. How it is used by the business, what analytics they can apply to make better business decisions and how they can use the information to influence their future and a customer's decision making process. Take an open-minded approach to technology, work with expert suppliers who can help you arrive at a bespoke solution which facilitates business growth, and you should get ahead of the competition.

By applying the above steps you can change the way you source and negotiate with potential ICT suppliers. It is critical that you stop and take the time to evaluate what steps you need to take and how they can help you reach your goals. Do this in your own time and do not rush towards change for change's sake.

Change your mindset from:

What do I need?

To:

What I need is!

Alan says:

This chapter is really all about mind-set change (see Suzanne Hazelton's chapter on this issue). How do you envisage the benefits to be derived from ICT, rather than simply getting by with your existing system on a 'make do and mend' basis.

Shakeeb identifies first the key business issues his clients face, such as poor cash flow and inadequate sales leads, and determines how the ICT solution can improve these areas for the client, not just now but on a longer term basis.

If you can take a broader view of your business and how ICT issues gel with your business plans, you will be in better shape to determine for yourself what systems you need rather than exposing yourself to an over specified system when you ask. 'What system do I need?' It puts control back in your own hands.

You may need help to do this but at the same time you need to discipline yourself to stick to your business objectives. Clients often see new applications for their system as it is developed to the extent that they become dependent on a legacy system for longer than they need to. There is only one person left who can understand it and make it work for them. Maybe future-proofing is too ambitious a concept but stay as flexible as you can so that any upgrades can be added sequentially.

When you are ready for a completely new system you will have a clear idea of what specification you will need.

CHOOSE YOUR EXIT STRATEGY

Antony Doggwiler

> Once an owner decides to retire the business folds, as without the owner's involvement there is little of value to sell on to provide a pension fund, unless...

Choose your exit strategy

A great business – what are you looking to do with it?

When it comes to exiting a business there are two types of entrepreneur. The first is one who had deliberately set out to create their business with an exit in mind. They have probably already been through the process before and have crafted the business plan for their new enterprise based on an expected exit value in a fixed number of years' time. They will also probably have co-investors who have involved themselves with the same end goal in mind. Therefore the business will be run with the exit in mind from day one.

The second type of entrepreneur who looks to exit their business is often somebody who has created something that is successful by accident. That is not intended to be derogatory, as this person is obviously a talented and hard-working individual with good commercial business skills. However, when they started their business their motivation was to create a good business rather than secure the best exit from it.

To a certain extent this chapter is targeted more at the second type above, somebody who knows that they have created a good business that has some value and who is making a good living from that business. However, they are equally conscious that they cannot go on forever and need to consider what is going to happen once they are no longer involved. More importantly, they need to know how they can realise a sizeable cash sum to secure their future.

A nice lifestyle or a pension fund?

Yes we know the answer is ideally both! However, many entrepreneurial businesses often sit in the former camp in that the business provides a good lifestyle in terms of earnings and enjoyment, but is maybe not best placed to provide a pension once the owner has ceased to work in the business.

An example of this is a small consultancy or trade business. The owner loves doing what they do and interacting with the customers. They may have a few employees that assist particularly on the administrative support side. Because of the particular skill that the owner has, they are able to charge premium prices and thus can enjoy a pretty healthy financial reward. However, once the owner decides that they want to be retire, the business folds, as without the owner's involvement there is little of value to sell on to provide a pension fund.

Surprisingly, well at least to their owners, larger businesses with many employees also fall into this category. Yes, there are teams of good sales, operations and administration people within the business but the key lynchpin of the whole enterprise is the owner manager. They drive the strategy, make the major decisions, control the key relationships and generally hold the whole thing together. Again they make very good money as a result. However, should the owner wish to leave the business, any potential value is significantly reduced as much of it will exit along with the owner.

This issue is very common in owner managed businesses, and unless it is recognised and dealt with, many entrepreneurs who think their businesses are worth millions will be sorely disappointed as this perceived worth is based primarily on their input, which of course will be lost to the business once they make their exit.

Do I have to sell my business in order to exit it?

It is not impossible to create a pension fund from a lifestyle or owner dependent business, though it does mean that the business effectively has to be run aggressively for profits and cash, particularly during its latter stages. The business value effectively has to be extracted while the owner is able and willing to work in the business and put aside elsewhere to provide income in retirement.

Following this path would mean that the business may end up being wound down, which will involve an exit cost, although it may be possible to sell a scaled down version of the business, perhaps to the employees or another individual in a similar field looking to expand their business. However, it is assumed that most business owners will be looking to exit their business via a sale and the remainder of the chapter is based on this scenario.

So where do I start?

One of the most popular newsletter articles that I ever produced was entitled "How to exit your business – in three years' time." The point that I was looking to make was that selling a business for maximum value is a process that takes years rather than months and one that needs to be started long before the search for a potential buyer commences.

The start point is the recognition by a business owner that there will need to be an exit at some point in the future. As noted above, this can be from day one of a business idea, but more usually it is a result of either an unsolicited offer to buy the business, a personal event such as illness or a landmark birthday, or a gradual realisation that you as an owner manager cannot, or do not want to, continue working for ever.

Once you realise you have to start to think about selling your business then you can start to focus on what needs to be done to prepare for exit. The end goal is normally a business that does not require your involvement that can be sold for the price that would enable you to do what you want to do once you have left the business.

Reliable financial data is a key starting point. Yes I know that I, as a finance person, would say that, but where large sums of money are involved, profits and cash are going to be closely scrutinised, and a thorough understanding of what they really are and how they are achieved is essential. The standard of financial and management reporting that a potential acquirer normally expects to see is often of a much higher quality than that which many entrepreneurs use to manage and monitor their business.

For example, a company that I was working with had been extremely successful in its chosen niche and the owners had been doing well financially. However, management information was limited, and the business relied on its own sense of what was profitable, backed up by a reasonable bank balance and a set of statutory accounts at the end of each year which justified the cash taken out of the business without paying too much tax. However, it was extremely difficult to demonstrate how much money the business was actually making and the potential for profit for each of its business lines going forward. By sitting down with the management team to examine the business model, reconciling it back to the financial books and records, as well as doing some benchmarking with other similar businesses, it was possible to construct a financial model that clearly demonstrated how profits were made and cash generated. This was then used to put in place a financial planning system that enable reliable future forecasts to be made, which proved to be extremely useful when potential purchasers came knocking.

Once you are happy that your financials are sound and that you fully understand the drivers of profit and cash, then you can seriously revisit and update your strategy and business plan. Your aim is ultimately to create the best business that you can in line with your end goal.

You also need to address the people side of the business. Your initial focus should be identifying how what you currently do within the business would be dealt with once you are gone. Succession planning is not just for family firms handing over to the next generation. Do the individuals already exist who will be able lead and manage the business in your absence? Who do you need to ensure remains in the business after you have left? These questions and more will need to be addressed as part of your exit planning.

Some internal due diligence also needs to be undertaken. Are your processes and documentation compliant with the various laws and regulations that exist? Do they minimise risk and protect the value of the business?

A number of these steps are discussed in more detail below. However, a decision to start the exit programme, regardless of when the proposed exit date actually is, is often the catalyst for putting in place a number of actions that actually improve the business and enhance its value. In short it is never too early to think about your business exit strategy. And your exit does not have to be in three years' time. It could be much shorter or a lot longer. It is how and when you plan for it that matters.

What if there is more than one of me?

This is a reference to the fact that a business may have more than one owner rather than any psychiatric medical condition. The main target of this section has been an individual owner manager. Nevertheless it is recognised that many entrepreneurial businesses do have more than one owner, often because of the complementary skills and experience of the individuals involved.

However, different people with different skills often have different aspirations. Whilst joint owners might think that their end goals for the business are the same, it is not unusual when it comes to the crunch for one or more of the parties involved to decide that their timescale for exit differs from that of their partners. It is possible to put in place an exit strategy that takes into account a range of different options, and much of the advice in this section remains valid for multiple exits. However, it does bring in an extra level of complexity that will need to be taken into account.

Hopefully you will already have a shareholders' or partnership agreement in place that can deal with any areas of tension that might arise in the run up to a business exit. If not this is probably something that should be dealt with as a matter of urgency.

It is all about people...

The decision to exit a business does not just impact on the owners. Fellow directors, minority shareholders, management, employees, customers, suppliers, trusted advisors and family members are also deeply affected. Most people are very conservative (with a small "c") when it comes to change and a new owner of the business that you are involved in is up near the top of situations most likely to cause stress and anxiety.

So who should be told and when? Very few people at the start as you are still formulating your exit strategy. As it begins to impact on each of the various parties you can start to involve them in your plans. Trusted advisors and close family (but note the comment re family businesses below) should be involved at an early stage as you will need their help, advice and support to get the process going and keep it on track.

As mentioned above, succession planning is a must. In order to maximise value there needs to be a future without you, so you have to have the people in place who will continue in the roles that you have been fulfilling. You will probably already be at the stage where you have a management team of sorts in your business. Hopefully it is a good team, a team that you have trust in, who can carry out their roles without your involvement, and can act upon their own initiative within the authority structures you have put in place. Ideally there will be a few individuals who you believe, perhaps with further development and training, have the ability to run, and more importantly grow, the business once you have gone.

If you have reached this stage, great, you can probably bring them into your confidence about your intentions reasonably well in advance of your exit. If you are some way away from this position then you need to be moving towards it fairly quickly. If you do not have suitable people in the business then you need to recruit them.

Sometimes when key employees hear that their boss is looking to sell their business, they immediately indicate that they would like to buy it via a management buy-out (MBO). This can be a good option in certain circumstances but it rarely leads to the achievement of the best price for your business. Therefore it is important not to get management hopes up unless you are really serious about selling to them. It is an easy and quick way to alienate and demotivate them at a time when you really need them to be on your side.

A better way would be to ensure that their interests are aligned with yours by introducing a suitable share scheme, such as the tax efficient Enterprise Management Incentive (EMI) scheme. This will enable them to personally benefit from the proceeds of any business sale. It may mean that you give up a percentage of your company, subject to certain conditions being met and targets being achieved, but the additional value that engaged and supportive employees can generate will more than compensate for this.

With major customers and suppliers, if win-win deals can be struck without compromising the attractiveness or value of the business then this should be done. Depending on relationships they can be informed of your intentions either before or after sale, based on what is best to ensure that they are willing to deal with the new owners.

A quick word about what are commonly known as "family businesses". It is true to say that in most entrepreneurial enterprises there is some family involvement, be it through initial loan capital or shareholding, or some admin or professional support. However "family businesses" tend to have a wider or deeper involvement of family members, often in key roles within the business. Therefore a decision to exit and the planning that follows will be more complex and possibly very emotional. Exiting these businesses would justify a chapter in their own right and is possibly outside the scope of this book. However much, of the advice in this chapter remains pertinent to "family businesses".

Dealing with people in business can be challenging at the best of times. During the exit process these people issues can multiply considerably. An understanding of everybody's position and expectations allied to clear and timely communication should help you to deal with most of the problems that could arise.

Getting the numbers and business plan right...

One of the biggest signs that a business sale has not been thought out is a poor quality offer document or information memorandum for sale. This kind of document invariably includes what is known as a "hockey stick" financial projection promising significantly increased profits and cash within three to five years' time. These forecasts often bear little or no resemblance to the historical numbers or underlying financial performance of the business.

Not surprisingly, producing the right kind of financial business plan starts well before the sale process begins. High quality management and financial reporting systems need to put in place if they are not already there. Reliable historical management accounts and robust budgeting and forecasting processes will give credibility to any financial information that is presented. If a business has a history of doing these things well, a potential purchaser will find it much harder to challenge the numbers.

If the numbers make sense then it is much easier to construct a business plan that explains how the business will continue to grow profitably under new ownership. It is true that most potential purchasers, when looking at a business plan, will look at market, people and financial numbers in that order. A good business has to understand the markets that it operates in and have products and services that are consistently in demand as well as the people who can consistently deliver them profitably. However, it is ultimately cash returns that count, so if the financials can be shown to be a sensible reflection of the underlying business then achieving the desired sale price will be that much easier.

Looking for skeletons…

This probably does not apply to you as all your paperwork is in order, all your client relationships are fully documented, your intellectual property is secured, and all your statutory compliance work is up to date. However, even in the best run businesses there will be areas that are not quite as clean and tidy as they should be.

This is not to say that anything illegal or dodgy is going on, it is just that time and resources often dictate that not all "i"s are dotted and "t"s crossed. There could also be potential warranty or guarantee issues or legal claims that sadly arise in the course of business and need to be kept on top of in order to minimise their impact.

A construction business that I became involved in had been fairly diligent in documenting key commercial agreements. However, the company books had not been kept up to date and key legal documents relating to shares and ownership were proving difficult to locate. By using one of our checklists it was possible to identify what was missing and what needed tidying up. The cost of doing this was more than compensated for by the additional value that was protected from challenge by a potential purchaser should any omissions have come to light during the due diligence process.

Identifying and dealing with these skeletons at an early stage should be a priority once a decision has been made to exit the business. The initial discussions about price are often based on top level information and an assumption that there are no real problems lurking within the business.

Once heads of terms have been agreed and due diligence commences (see below) there is only one way the price can go (downwards for the avoidance of doubt), and if problems are revealed when a purchaser digs deeper into the business they will want to renegotiate. By being upfront with yourself and your advisors about potential problems and dealing with them, you are in a much stronger position to resist pressure to reduce the price.

Therefore it is often a good idea to undertake your own internal due diligence exercise prior to starting the sale process so that problems can be dealt with before they affect the value of the business.

Elsewhere in this book you will find details of the range of legal issues that all entrepreneurs need to be aware of and keep on top of. By doing so you will make the sale process so much easier to get through and minimise the potential for disruption.

Who are my potential buyers and what are they looking for?

If you were to be asked who could buy your business I am sure you could immediately list a number of companies who would be interested. I guess they would primarily be competitors or perhaps that large major player who would like to get into your sector. Most owners think in terms of what are known as trade buyers when considering the sale of their business, and such buyers are often interested and in a good position to conclude a deal.

You would think that a trade buyer would offer the best option in terms of maximising the price but that is not necessarily true. A trade buyer's view of the future potential of your business is often restricted by the fact that their experience is limited to the sectors in which they operate.

Therefore there are sometimes richer pickings to be had from what is known as a strategic investor. Examples of strategic investors are businesses operating in a sector that has links to yours and who may have a complementary offering that would work in both sectors. This also applies to businesses, particularly from overseas, who are looking to enter into your market. This type of buyer can sometimes see a bigger picture and may be prepared to pay well in order to achieve their strategic aims.

I recently spoke with an entrepreneur who was convinced that only businesses in the UK would be interested in purchasing his business. However, after some discussions with corporate finance advisors it emerged that his area of specialisation could be very attractive to companies from the USA and India who were looking to break into the UK and then use it as a springboard into continental Europe. Work is now being undertaken to ensure that the business is properly positioned to take advantage of such interest.

If your business is still at a relatively early stage, with high growth potential that you as an owner manager recognise is beyond your experience and finances, then a financial investor could be an option. In this case it is down to you if you want to stay along for the ride or not.

A management buy-out, as mentioned above, is a possibility, particularly in a people based business, and this can be achieved tax efficiently over a reasonably short period of time. Another possibility along the same lines is a management buy-in, whereby an experienced executive or perhaps an executive team buy themselves into the business. They effectively take over the management role that the existing owner is undertaking, as well as their shares in the business. This approach may not offer top dollar as regards sale price, but can be a good option if there is a lack of obvious trade buyers or strategic investors.

Although some advisors might tell you otherwise, selling a business is like selling any other product or service. You need to understand the market for your business and who you might be selling to. You have to be aware of its unique selling points and what makes it different from anybody else. You also need to be aware of its value, both to yourself, and more importantly, to a potential purchaser.

It is also important to note that whoever is buying your business is buying its future. I hesitate to push this point too strongly as, human nature being what it is, the past often plays a far greater role in a purchaser's decision than it should. However, although your past results may be impressive, attention does need to be paid to detailing your sustainable cash profits in any financial forecasts that are prepared. Clear explanations need to be provided as to the drivers of these profits and, most importantly, why they will continue and grow under a new owner.

Equally, be aware that when a potential buyer is buying the future of your business it is also calculating what it can add to the value through its own efforts. This could be through cost savings, process synergies, market consolidation or increased selling opportunities. This is something that you and your advisors should also be thinking of, as it is a part of the value that an acquirer places on your business, and something that you might also want a part of as your price for selling. Understanding the motivation of your buyer is the key to obtaining maximum value for your business.

Opportunistic sales

One thing that often focuses the mind on an exit is the "opportunistic offer". This is where a business owner receives an unsolicited enquiry about the possibility of selling their business. What do you do if you do suddenly find yourself with somebody knocking on your door willing to purchase your business?

Well it's not actually about what you should do. It is about what you should already have done. To a certain extent a business should already be sales ready. Its financial systems and processes should be in good shape. Its skeletons as noted above, should already have been identified and addressed. Its people should be talented, well trained and motivated.

Most importantly, you as a business owner should not actually be surprised that you have received such an offer because your mind should already be attuned to the possibility of an exit.

One owner manager I know received an approach to buy their business from a major corporate. On the face of it they seemed to be offering a reasonable sum of money, and the owner freely admitted that if such an offer had been made a year or so before he would have happily taken it. However, because he had started to plan for his exit, he was able to assess the offer more critically and see that it was not as good as it appeared to be, in that it undervalued the business significantly as well as imposing onerous earn-out clauses. He therefore turned the offer down and has subsequently seen his business continue to grow in sales, profitability and, most importantly, in value.

Often an opportunistic offer can seem extraordinarily attractive. Sometimes it genuinely is. However you can only know whether it is or isn't if you have already given your exit some thought and have already started your initial actions.

Doing the deal

Once a decision has been made to sell, the next challenge is to do so without disruption to the smooth running of the business. Selling a business is virtually a full time job, and therefore it is important to have as much of a dedicated resource as you can afford.

It is also a very protracted process, particularly when you are a small or medium sized business. You will start with some discussions with your selected advisors. You will then need to work on an information package which will be used to market the business. Once some potential purchasers have been identified you will have a series of meetings with these before finally selecting one (or sometimes more) to have more serious discussion with.

You need to check that any potential purchasers are genuine buyers and are not just trying to find out sensitive information about your business for their own benefit. You also need to make sure that they are able to finance the deal by seeking detailed information as to where the cash to buy your business is going to come from.

The short-listed candidates will require more information before you finally settle on a purchaser and a price. Heads of terms will need to be agreed before the purchaser then carries out due diligence. This will involve a detailed examination of all aspects of your company, covering legal documentation, financial history and forecasts, and market and commercial issues.

Assuming this does not reveal any major problems then you will move on to the sale and purchase agreement. This will turn your heads of agreement into a full package of legal documentation including the main contract, supporting information and any warranties or indemnities that may be agreed.

Purchasers will ask for warranties and indemnities so that they can go back to you for compensation if something emerges after they bought the business that, had they been aware of prior to purchase, might have meant that they would not have done the deal or alternatively would have paid a lower price. You can resist giving any but it could mean that you end up with less money. A better approach is to ensure you understand and fully disclose any risks as early as possible in the exit process, and work with your advisors to manage these.

One issue that will probably arise is whether you sell your company or the business, assets and liabilities within that company. If you sell the company you are selling everything to do with that company including any problems that may later emerge. Obviously, for a purchaser this is high risk, and to mitigate this risk they may ask for a number of more onerous warranties and indemnities as well and seek to pay a lower price. If they just buy the business and not the company, then their risk is reduced, which may be reflected in the price. However, you will be left to deal with the winding up of the company. There may also be tax implications to consider.

It is a balancing act and one that you will need your accountants and lawyers to be on top of and advise you accordingly. Equally it is a negotiation process, and you are perfectly at liberty to hold out for what you believe is the right deal for you.

There are a number of professional advisors that you will need to involve in the process. Chief among these will be accountants and lawyers. Sadly, the accountants or lawyers who have helped you grow your business may not be the best people to help you to sell it, however much they will say they can. It is a specialist area, particularly on the tax side, and therefore you need to involve people with experience of doing deals in your sector and with the various parties involved.

You will also probably need somebody to help you market and sell your business. There are firms who specialise in this area, particularly in the SME and owner managed business sector, so examine a number of options, their areas of expertise, and their terms of business, before deciding who is best placed to help you.

Other consultants that could usefully be involved include interim or part-time managers who can manage the process within the business, thus reducing the stresses and strains on yourself and your management team and minimising any negative impact on the business.

Who you ultimately choose depends on the personnel involved. If you have been successful in business, you will have already developed a good instinct for people and whether they can deliver. Just because you are dealing with highly paid professionals it does not mean that you should put your trust in them without doing some due diligence of your own.

Another issue to decide on is how much competition you should encourage in the bidding process and how long you should keep each bidder involved. In theory more competition should up the price, but such a process needs to be handled carefully. You will eventually go exclusively with one party but it is good to have a back-up option in case the sale to the preferred bidder does not work out.

Believe it or not, the above only scratches the surface of what is involved. You will experience all manner of frustrations during the sale process. You may get one or two false starts.

You will find yourself occasionally wondering why you are bothering. However, you are not alone and with determination, perseverance and the right level of support you eventually reach the point when all parties finally sign on the dotted line and you will have successfully achieved what you set out to do – exit your business.

Afterwards…

That's it! You've sold up and are ready to sail off into the sunset. And yet are you really ready to make that clean break from something that you have put so much of your life into?

To a certain extent you may have no choice. Some of the purchase consideration may be in the form of shares in the new business or dependent on an earn-out, whereby some of the sale cash is linked to future profits.

Earn-outs are understandably very popular with purchasers as it enables them to hedge their bets to a certain extent by making some of the payment performance related. However, from a seller's side they can be difficult to make work as once the business is sold, control and management of the business is lost, and however many safeguards are put in place it is difficult to get a real handle on true post-sale profitability. It also means that the seller continues to have an involvement in the business whether they want to or not.

Aside from the above financial ties, remaining involved depends on how hands-on you have been with the business in the last years of ownership. If you have been virtually a non-executive chairman mentoring and guiding a strong management team, then remaining as a non-executive in the newly owned business is a possibility.

Where you still have some specialist knowledge or key client relationships, a consultancy arrangement could be useful for both sides. However, the seller has to recognise that this is a new relationship with the business and resist temptation to meddle in areas that they no longer have responsibility for or be a hulking presence in the background distracting the new management team's efforts to move the business forward.

Experience suggests that a clean break is often the best for all involved, but as ever it depends on the personalities involved and the business set-up post-sale.

So there you are. You have your cash. Your future is as secure as it can be. What do you do? Maybe you will be able to devote your life to good works and leisure. Or maybe you will want to do it all over again. Whatever you decide, you can do so in the knowledge that through proper preparation and planning you achieved the best exit from your current business that you could, and that you are now in control of your own destiny. Isn't that a good place to be in?

Alan says:

Antony emphasises that it takes three years from the decision to sell to prepare for the maximum value to be achieved.

Such a timetable puts into perspective the other vital elements for a high performance business included in this book. These include having a clear vision for the future of the business and being able to manage profitable growth effectively by judicious application of modern marketing techniques and thinking.

If you have also developed a good experience of presenting your business to money lenders (sorry, financial institutions) you will be better prepared for the arduous process of selling your business that Antony describes.

It is worth noting, as Antony highlights, that the highest bids do not always come from the most obvious quarters.

Opening up markets as your business may well have done, and introducing a range of products successfully and competitively into that market, is an expensive and time consuming process which carries with it a high perceived value from certain strategic investors.

AUTHOR PROFILES

Alan Charlesworth

Alan's business, and his passion, is helping entrepreneurs to create high performance business.

Sometimes entrepreneurs, such as yourself, can struggle to achieve the goals you started out with. Alan works with you and your team to re-examine objectives and strategy and create a plan to bridge the gap between where you are and where you want to be.

This process helps you get to grips with 'difficult to resolve', business-critical issues and kick-start growth plans to achieve your longer term goals. These may include a successful exit strategy.

Alan's experience with multinationals such as Johnson & Johnson, in CEO roles including Mintel International, now a transatlantic Super Brand, and on many consultancy projects provides a strong platform to help you achieve new levels of performance.

Has your business plateaued, causing you frustration and sleepless nights and are you seeking help in recapturing your company's growth curve?

Alan's experience in such situations will help you develop a clear plan for the future with enthusiasm and confidence.

Alan is known for transforming his client's business and leaving them excited by its future prospects.

For further information about my work with clients my website is www.alakarconsulting.com

Find me on Facebook at
http://www.facebook.com/alan.charlesworth.54

Find me on Twitter: https://twitter.com/alanrcharles

See more about my professional credentials on LinkedIn
http://www.linkedin.com/in/alanrcharlesworth

To contact me for a no obligation discussion, email me at:
alan@alakarconsulting.com

Maurice Cheng

Maurice started his career as a research consultant, gathering market evidence to help clients grow in their markets. Getting into Board Marketing roles gave him the opportunity to use market understanding to work within a business to drive revenues. Along the way however came the realisation that defining good opportunities and goals was a lot easier than delivering them – staff had a way of getting in the way at times. Then came the understanding that, actually, working with managers and staff to define the vision and objectives in the first place meant strategies were understood and delivered as a team much more easily.

Maurice works for his clients in executive and non-executive roles, in a mix of commercial, public sector and not for profit companies in the UK, Europe and North America.

It's not a branded formula, it is an approach that works, for entrepreneurs, company directors and non-executives who believe their organisation needs to grow, and change to grow – and grow its people along with it.

Interested in having a first discussion about how Maurice could help work with you and your managers to define and drive growth?

See more about my professional credentials on LinkedIn: http://www.linkedin.com/in/mauricecheng

To contact me for a no obligation discussion email me at: maurice@cheng.co.uk

Suzanne Hazelton

Suzanne describes herself as a peopleologist, working with individuals and organisations to THRIVE!

Suzanne is passionate about working with people and organisations to "be the best". However in her experience successful people, such as yourself, achieve success and then often plateau and don't become all that you and your business are capable of becoming. This problem manifests itself in two distinct ways:

Firstly perhaps you want 'more' but find it difficult to articulate or to know how to take it to the next level. This can leave you, and those working around you, feeling disconnected and less motivated. This negatively impacts not only on your happiness but also the business's bottom line.

Alternatively, perhaps you know your 'game changing' idea, but have difficulty developing it, whether through fear, lack of focus or an inability to articulate it clearly.

Suzanne's an experienced coach and trainer, and works both with corporate leaders and with entrepreneurs, like yourself. She's got a Master's degree in Applied Positive Psychology, training in NLP and psychotherapy – all tools which she can use to enable you to unlock whatever's holding you back, enabling you to build on your success and achieve transformational results.

Suzanne is the author of two books, *Raise Your Game: How to build on your results to achieve transformational results* and *Great Days at Work: How positive psychology can transform your working life.*

If your business has plateaued and is causing you frustration and sleepless nights you may want to consider re-invigorating yourself, in order to spark business growth.

Suzanne is known for leaving people feeling zestified and ready for the bigger game.

Find me on Facebook at
http://www.facebook.com/suzannehazelton1

Find me on Twitter: https://twitter.com/suzannehazelton

See my videos on YouTube:
http://www.youtube.com/user/suzannehazelton

See more about my professional credentials on LinkedIn:

http://www.linkedin.com/in/suzannehazelton

To contact me for a no obligation discussion, email me at: Suzanne@johnsonfellowes.co.uk

Peter Kelly FInst SMM

Peter has worked with entrepreneurs for the last 11 years. He helps them identify and secure the appropriate funding for their needs. His clients are at all stages of their development, from start-up, through growth and even at the turnaround stage. He provides all types of both equity and debt funding.

Peter Kelly co-founded Pegasus Funding Resources to specialise in helping start-up and growth companies to prepare themselves for funding and introduce them to sources of finance. In particular Peter uses his experience to guide companies through the business plan writing process and the challenge of not only presenting to investors but of being well prepared for the unexpected questions that will follow.

He has more than 30 years of corporate experience, including European Managing Director and European Vice President roles, in leading companies in the Multimedia, Document and Training Management, Online Auctions, Telecommunications and Global Sourcing sectors. His experience encompasses the creation of start-up operations right through to final IPO or trade sale.

For further information about my work with clients my website is:

http://www.pegasusfunding.co.uk

See more about my professional credentials on LinkedIn:
http://www.linkedin.com/pub/peter-kelly

Find me on Twitter: https://twitter.com/peterekelly

To contact me for a no obligation discussion email me at:
Peter.kelly@pegasusfunding.co.uk

Toby Stroh

Toby specialises in helping entrepreneurs in start-ups and small to mid-size businesses in sectors as diverse as hi-tech university spin-outs and property as well as leisure and financial services. His experience ranges from venture capital, private equity and capital markets work involving fundraising and investor exits, to major project work and mergers and acquisitions.

He heads up the Company Commercial team at Druces LLP, a City of London law firm, as well its Entrepreneurs' Group, a specialist sector group working across the firm in commercial, employment, taxation and property and litigation matters.

The Entrepreneurs' Group advises clients on the structuring of new ventures, commercial matters such as guarantees, finance agreements, shareholders agreements and joint ventures, as well as dealing with a broad range of related matters including third party investments and exit and succession planning.

Toby also leads Druces LLP's membership of the Alliance of Business Lawyers, a dynamic worldwide organisation of law firms with an international clientele which greatly assists internationally minded entrepreneurs with global aspirations. Druces LLP, based in Moorgate, has 17 partners specialising in the full range of corporate and private client disciplines. It is a dynamic and innovative business, which actively seeks new opportunities for expansion through new appointments and mergers.

For further information about my work with clients my website is: http://www.druces.com

See more about my professional credentials on LinkedIn: http://www.linkedin.com/pub/toby-stroh

To contact me for a no obligation discussion email me at: info@druces.com

Victoria Ash & Paul Griffith

Victoria and Paul are partners in RCR, helping entrepreneurial businesses to grow their revenue through a combination of consulting, coaching and hands-on support.

Victoria Ash

Victoria has a track record of helping entrepreneurial businesses grow, as well as working with a wide variety of major corporates, mid-tier businesses and professional services organisations to improve their positioning, marketing, sales and communication.

Victoria's experience covers a wide range of business-to-business sectors and typical engagements include helping senior management to define marketing strategy and set budgets; acting as an outsourced marketing director; coaching individual partners and managers in building their revenue; and devising and implementing successful marketing and PR campaigns.

Paul Griffith

Paul has run his own small and mid-sized businesses and has held management and consulting positions in the corporate world at Unilever and Coopers & Lybrand (now PwC).

Paul enjoys creativity and being thorough. In the business world this shows up as creating sustainable market positions for businesses and shaping the business processes that deliver on these promises. It also means seeing things through from concept to implementation.

For further information about our work with clients our website is: www.rcrpartnership.com

Find us on Twitter at: https://twitter.com/RCRgrowsSMEs
See more about our professional credentials on LinkedIn:
http://uk.linkedin.com/in/victoriaash
http://uk.linkedin.com/in/pdpgriffith

Or email us to start a conversation at:
vash@rcrpartnership.com
pgriffith@rcrpartnership.com

Shakeeb Niazi

An entrepreneur with significant experience and expertise in information technology and a passion for helping small enterprises realise their potential. Owner of several companies that provide innovative technological solutions to develop businesses, expand their customer base and increase market share whilst also providing technical support services for their entire IT infrastructure.

He works with entrepreneurs seeking to enhance their business strategy with innovative, secure IT solutions as part of the growth and change management of their organisations.

Shakeeb specialises in IT projects at a senior level and is a technical solutions architect, business intelligence analyst and project manager, with nearly 30 years' experience in bringing technology-driven projects from conception to fruition. Major clients have included Dixons Retail Plc, OMV (Trading) UK, Performing Rights Society Ltd and the London Borough of Hammersmith and Fulham. He is a Chartered Information Technology Professional (CITP) with the British Computer Society and a mentor on their entrepreneurship programme.

Shakeeb's core businesses are: N-Tire Systems specialists in hardware, software and support; Ecomtastic, a digital marketing company, with solutions for SMEs requiring online strategies, branding and design; and DM4 Accountants, which is a new fresh-faced agency with the sole purpose of promoting accountants in their chosen location and generating pre-qualified leads.

See more about Shakeeb's professional credentials on LinkedIn: http://www.linkedin.com/in/shakeebniazi

For further information about our service offerings visit:
http://www.n-tiresystems.com
http://www.ecomtastic.com
http://www.dm4accountants.com

Just use the contact form for a no obligation discussion.

Antony Doggwiler

Antony's approach to business is simple – he takes care of the numbers so you don't have to.

Most entrepreneurs go into business because they love what they do. Whether marketing, selling, operating or inventing, it is their passion for what they believe they are good at that spurs them on.

Whilst obviously having a keen eye for profits and cash, most aspects of finance are something they endure rather than enjoy. That is fine at the start, but as a business grows finance invariably begins to take up more and more time.

This is where Antony's skills come to the fore as he quickly assesses what needs to be done and gets on with it, leaving the entrepreneur free to get on with what he enjoys, and more importantly, creates value for the business.

Because he has worked with both corporates and SMEs he is

able to bring that big business expertise while having empathy with the issues and challenges a growing business faces.

Working on a flexible basis Antony is able to start with a business earlier than the cost of a full time appointment would normally allow and can often continue working with the entrepreneur right up until an exit is achieved

The result – more money, more time, less hassle!

For further information about how myself and my colleagues can help look at our website: www.orchardgrowth.com

Find me on Twitter: https://twitter.com/antonydoggwiler

See more about my professional credentials on LinkedIn: http://www.linkedin.com/in/antonydoggwiler

To contact Antony for a no obligation discussion email: ajd@orchardgrowth.com

References

Chapter 3 – Suzanne Hazelton

Dweck, C. S. (2006). *Mindset: the new psychology of success.* New York: Random House

Frankl, V. E. (2004) *Man's search for meaning: the classic tribute to hope from the Holocaust.* London: Rider.

Rooke, D. & Torbert, W. R. (2005) Seven Transformations of Leadership. *Harvard Business Review.*

Chapter 7 – Shakeeb Niazi

http://en.wikipedia.org/wiki/PlayStation_Network_outage